When Prophets Spoke

23rd June 2023

Amazon UK

When Prophets Spoke

Spiritualism in the Old Testament

Rev. G. Maurice Elliott

PSYCHIC PRESS LTD.
20, EARLHAM STREET
LONDON, WC2H 9LW

First Published 1938
Second Edition 1940
This Edition 1987

ISBN 0 85384 069 5

Printed and bound in Great Britain
by Booksprint

PREFACE

This book is a serious attempt to *understand* the so-called miraculous and theophanic elements in the Old Testament.

When a thoughtful person hears a priest recite the words, "God spake these words, and said . . ." he naturally wants to know what is meant by the terms "God" and "spake." And if he is told that "God" means "The One Eternal God of the universe" and that "spake" means "uttered words," it is mere double-dutch to him because no man can *think* in such terms.

And, if he is told that "The Lord" had a long conversation with Abram and dined with him, he is quick to ask what is meant by the term "The Lord." He asks because such statements are meaningless to him if the term "The Lord" means "God."

How then, are we to understand such expressions as "God spake," "The Lord appeared," "The Angel said"? We must regard them either as the Easterner's pictorial way of describing his own intuitions and reasonings or as referring to spirit-messengers who were seen and heard.

The man who is well acquainted with physical science and biblical scholarship, but is ignorant of psychic science, is tied up to the "intuitions and reasonings" explanation.

No duly informed person to-day believes in miracle. There can be no arbitrary contravention of natural law.

The Old Testament, then, is full of *supernormal* phenomena, not supernatural or miraculous.

The so-called supernatural of to-day is the natural of to-morrow. We live in a natural, spiritual world. The natural and the spiritual interpenetrate. Spiritual law is natural; natural law is spiritual. That is why no one can say where natural law ends and spiritual law begins. Sir Oliver Lodge writes: "Conspicuously does the Bible maintain the constant activity of divine agents everywhere as testified to by supernormal occurrences."

The author has been fortunate. For many years he has been in constant contact with discarnate human beings in what is called "The Other World." He, and tens of thousands like him, can therefore *think* in terms in which the average person cannot *yet* think.

Studying the Bible, with this new set of psychic terms in which to think, he has found that what men thought to be pictorial descriptions of intuitions and reasonings, are obviously meant to describe objective manifestations of spirit-guides.

He has also found that such terms as "God," "Angel," "Angel of the Lord," "Spirit" and "man" are sometimes used interchangeably.

He believes that "Yahweh" was the name of the supreme spirit-guide of the Patriarchs and the Hebrews. He was one of God's messengers whose aim it was to lead men to a true conception of God. In order to do this he had to act and speak with the authority of a vicegerent.

The Hebrews were an idolatrous people who needed "a human image to adore," a spirit-guide who could *materialize* and be seen and heard and spoken to. They could not, in the early stages, rise to the conception

"God is Spirit." Later, however, when Yahweh had trained them sufficiently, they began to look beyond Yahweh the spirit-guide to Yahweh the One Eternal God.

One of the chief causes of the neglect of Bible-study has been, and still is, the Church's refusal to face facts. She will not face the facts of Spiritualism though she knows that vast numbers of the *intelligent* members of the Church are reading the writings of Lodge, Crookes, Barrett, and a host of other students of Psychic Science.

Men are fast out-growing the cruder dogmas and doctrines of the Church, and its ignorant interpretation of the miraculous and theophanic elements in Scripture; and, having been brought up to regard the Church and the Bible as inseparable, they have little use for the Bible. They are not interested.

The Bible was written by Spiritualists—even though they did not call themselves by that name. It is a psychical or Spiritualistic book from cover to cover. Its narratives are mainly Spiritualistic. They deal with visions, voices, dreams, trance, materialization, dematerialization, levitation, automatic-writing, mediums, spiritual healings and so forth. This will become transparently clear to any one who will seriously study the Bible.

The author trusts that those who may honour him by looking into his book will bear in mind that it consists of a series of articles which appeared in *Psychic News*. Some slight alterations have been made, but the somewhat blunt and racy form remains.

Above all he trusts that his readers will be patient and tolerant of his serious attempt to *understand* the psychic narratives of the Old Testament.

It is not possible to thank all those from whose friendship and writings he has received instruction and enlightenment. But, when he remembers all that he owes to them, the words come into his mind, "What have I that I have not received."

CONTENTS

CHAPTER I

The writers of the Bible take it for granted that spirit-intercourse and other psychical phenomena are well known to their readers. The writer of the story of Adam and Eve informs his readers that they were clairaudient and held converse with a spirit named Yahweh. It matters not, for our purpose, whether Adam and Eve lived or not.

We may, however, note in passing that "Adam" is a plural Hebrew word meaning "Mankind," and that "Eve" means "Life." "Male and female created He them and called *their* name Adam," i.e., Mankind. The story is "truth embodied in a tale"—the truth that Life tempts males and females to do good and evil.

The early writers of the Bible evidently knew that their readers were familiar with the psychical phenomenon of clairaudience—otherwise this story, and the stories following, would have been meaningless.

The author of the Epistle to the Hebrews writes, "By faith Abraham, when he was called, obeyed . . . and he went out not knowing whither he went."

What caused Abram to have faith? The "Call," undoubtedly. What was the nature of the "Call"? It was a *definite, objective psychical manifestation.* It was *not* a subjective spiritual experience.

Here are the facts: In the twelfth chapter of Genesis we read that the Lord, which means a spirit, *spoke* to Abram, who, being clairaudient, *heard* him. This spirit told him to leave his home, his kindred and his country, promising to guide him to another land, where he would become the father of a great nation. A drastic injunction if ever there were one!

But Abram—the Spiritualist—was neither surprised nor doubtful, and he obeyed the "Call."

"So Abram went as the Lord had spoken unto him" and took with him Sarah, his wife, and Lot, his nephew, his servants and slaves, sheep and oxen—indeed, "all their substance"—and journeyed to Canaan. Passing through that land he came to Shechem "unto the Oak of Moreh."

"Moreh" means "Soothsayer," which suggests that there had been an oracle belonging to it. An oracle was a place where men sought the advice and help of the spirit world, where questions were asked and the answers given through a medium, seer, prophet, prophetess, sensitive or whatever name is preferred.

It was amid such psychic surroundings that Abram's clairvoyant powers were brought into play. He *saw* his spirit guide, "the Lord *appeared* unto Abram, and said, Unto thy seed will I give this land." We do not wonder that Abram, realizing the psychic atmosphere of the place, built there an altar.

The original purpose of altars was that they might serve as a means by which men could be brought into contact with the gods, that is, with spirits. An altar was regarded as a temporary abode of the communicating spirit. These ancient writers appear to have been fully acquainted with that which Spiritualists know so well.

Throughout his life, certainly for many years, Abram received counsel and guidance from his spirit communicator.

Abram did not live "by faith alone." He had definite objective psychical evidence, and it was on that evidence that he based and exercised his faith.

As we pursue our study of the psychic stories we shall find that neither in the Old Testament nor in the New Testament did men live "by faith alone."

Abram continued his journey and reached "the mountain on the East of Bethel," where he again "built an altar unto the Lord" for the purpose of providing suitable conditions for "holding a sitting," as modern Spiritualists would say, and of "calling upon" or "getting into touch with" his spirit guide. It is more than likely that his guide had told him where and when to build an altar, and how best to hold converse with him.

None but a Spiritualist can hope to give even an approximately correct setting to the life of so great a clairaudient and clairvoyant as this psychically gifted "Father of the Faithful."

It is now time to ask, "Why did the Lord select or call Abram to be the founder of a great religious nation, and the recipient of heaven's blessing?" It cannot have been on account of his moral integrity, as the following story will show.

Abram in continuing his journey reached Judah, and, as there was a famine in the land, he went down to Egypt, for there would be "corn in Egypt" if anywhere.

When he arrived there he did not quite like the look of his wife, Sarah, for, though she was nearly seventy years of age, she was apparently as good-looking and as attractive as ever. Abram feared that the princes of Pharaoh, who were ever on the look out for desirable additions to their master's harem, would not be likely to miss Sarah "in a crowd."

Moreover, Abram feared that Sarah's entrancing beauty would lead the princes to kill him while saving her. So he persuaded her to say that she was not his wife, but his sister. A "very shabby trick" Mrs. Stobart calls it in her *Ancient Lights*.

Well, the princes did not miss seeing the beautiful Sarah, whom they speedily carried off to Pharaoh's house. He was delighted with the "find," and heaped wealth upon Abram.

Pharaoh made Sarah his wife. No blame can be attached to Pharaoh. Theoretically, all the wives of his subjects were his, and, I suppose, mere sisters doubly so. Abram alone was to blame.

Yet in spite of his "very shabby trick," he was a far better man than Pharaoh. So the Lord, knowing that only some desperate expedient could free Sarah, saw fit to inflict Pharaoh and his house with disease. This would lead Pharaoh to consult his magicians, who were probably psychic and able to reveal to him the truth about Sarah.

Pharaoh at once rebuked Abram, but, fearing to inflict punishment, he merely recalled Sarah from his harem and sent her back to the "Father of the Faithful," who had acted neither as a father nor as a man of faith.

It is clear, then, that Abram was not "called" by the Lord on account of his moral integrity. He was chosen, primarily, because he possessed psychic gifts, without which he could not have heard and seen his spirit communicator.

This does not imply that his mediumistic powers were in themselves a sufficient qualification for leadership, but it does imply that, given a general upright and religious character, a psychic endowment is indispensable for religious leadership.

Religion is revelation, and revelation can only be given to those who have the psychic capacity to receive it. It has always been so—in every religion. Abram's character is not to be judged by the one or two slips he made.

Fortunately for us all, the Father of spirits—the Greatest of Sportsmen—knows that the best of batsmen may *occasionally* be caught out in the slips first ball.

CHAPTER II

Abram, the Spiritualist, was the father of a great nation of Spiritualists. In the twelfth chapter of Genesis we found him exercising his clairaudient and clairvoyant powers, which enabled him to hear and see his spirit guide named Yahweh.

This guide told him to leave his own country, and promised to guide him to another land which he and his descendants would possess. We noted, too, how Abram used to build altars for the purpose of communicating with Yahweh, and how this great guide saved Sarah from remaining in Pharaoh's harem.

In Genesis xiii we find Abram, with his wife Sarah, and his nephew Lot, leaving Pharaoh's country and returning to—where?—"unto the place of the altar, which he had made in Canaan at the first."

The psychical conditions of that place were evidently conducive to spirit-intercourse, "and there Abram called on the name of the Lord." He certainly needed spirit guidance, for he was soon confronted with a grave difficulty.

Abram and Lot had each large flocks and herds and "the land was not able to bear them." Their herdsmen quarrelled. It was a question of water-supply. Arab tribes to-day quarrel over the wells.

Abram's solution was so extraordinarily generous that Spiritualists will find no difficulty in believing that his guide had told him how best to solve the problem.

Abram, being a Spiritualist, would naturally seek his guide's advice on so important an occasion, and we are not surprised to read, "and Abram said unto Lot, let there be no strife . . . if thou dost choose the left, I will go to the right, or, if thou dost choose the right, I will go to the left."

Lot chose the well-watered East; Abram had to be content with the West and was compensated by another visit from Yahweh, who promised him and his seed all the land he could see.

Abram then moved to Hebron and again built an altar to be the trysting-place between Yahweh and himself. Meanwhile Lot's greediness led to his being captured by invaders. Abram pursued and defeated them and rescued Lot.

Yahweh then came to Abram in the darkness. It was night. The stars were shining. Let the sceptic note that even Abram held spirit intercourse "in the dark." His guide assured him that he need have no fear, his reward would be "exceeding great."

But Abram urged his guide to remember that the reward he needed most was a son who should be heir to the exceeding greatness. He hated the thought of all his possessions passing to Dammesek Eliezer, who was not his son.

What a natural conversation! His guide did not

rebuke him for his lack of faith. He merely promised that Abram should have a son of his own body.

"And Abram believed Yahweh, and he counted it to him for righteousness." These words are really of great importance, because they are quoted by St. Paul as a proof-text for his doctrine of "justification by faith." Paul pointed his readers to Abram's exemplary faith.

But what kind of faith had Abram? What was the nature of it? Did he believe in the existence of Yahweh on hearsay evidence? Did he rely on faith alone when he left his own country, kindred and father's house to journey to Canaan?

Did he rest his assurance on faith alone that he would become the father of a great nation and be uniquely blessed? In a word, was Abram's faith similar to the faith of a man to-day who believes in "justification by faith"?

Certainly not. It had hardly anything in common with such a faith. Abram's faith was based on knowledge. He had seen, heard, and spoken to his spirit guide Yahweh. He had received direct, objective manifestation and revelation.

His faith was not based on "hearsay" evidence and subjective impression. It is true that his psychical experiences impressed him deeply and enabled him to exercise faith, but his faith was quite unlike the faith of church folk of to-day.

Consider, for example, Abram's reaction to Yahweh's promise that he should inherit the land of Canaan. He asked Yahweh, "How shall I *know* that I shall inherit it?" He required more than a promise—even from a denizen of another world.

And Yahweh did not rebuke him for having so inquiring a disposition, but readily turned the promise into a solemn compact, thus making it a certainty. If ever a man's faith was based on knowledge, Abram's was.

The words, "And Abram believed in Yahweh; and he counted it to him for righteousness" in no way support the doctrine of "justification by faith" any more than they support the rabbinical teaching that "Abram inherited this world and the world to come solely by the merit of faith," and that "God punishes more severely for doctrine than for practice."

We may pity those spiritually deaf and blind rabbis in their ignorance. But does not the Church maintain that, unless a man believe the Catholic Faith as expressed in the Athanasian Creed, he cannot be saved? And surely this is only another way of saying that unless a man believe the Church's official statement of doctrine he will be damned.

The famous evangelical text, "The just shall live by faith" does not mean anything like what it has been made to mean. It is a mis-translation.

The correct translation of what that great medium—the prophet Habakkuk—wrote is this: "The good man shall live by his faithfulness," which means, "the man who is faithful in all the relations of life, and is sincere and upright in heart and purpose, has in his character a principle of permanence."

Habakkuk, the Spiritualist, wrote what Spiritualists are teaching and writing to-day. Yet his words have been used to buttress a theological fortress of dogmas, doctrines, and threats! Is it not high time that we had a correct translation of the Bible?

Who is to do it? None but Spiritualists can do it. And such Spiritualists would have to be experts in biblical scholarship.

Our only hope is to convert at least some of the biblical scholars to Spiritualism. We shall then see them at work on the greatest Spiritualist literature in existence, and they will work in conjunction with their guides.

In that day we shall have a new Bible and a truly spiritual religion.

CHAPTER III

In the Bible, the words angel, Lord, man, God and spirit are sometimes used interchangeably to designate a spirit-visitant.

In the story of Hagar, for example, the spirit-visitant is called "the Lord" and also "the angel of the Lord." Spiritualists know that when a particular guide is unable to be with us he sends his "messenger."

In the sixteenth chapter of Genesis, we find Abram growing impatient about the unfulfilled promise made by his guide, Yahweh, that he and Sarah would have a son. No wonder! Abram had already waited ten years.

Ten years ago, he had *believed* what Yahweh had told him and "it was counted to him for righteousness." Abram was nearly a hundred years old, and Sarah was nearly ninety.

The old man was losing faith in his guide's promise, and his wife was evidently the victim of his complaining and grumbling. So she suggested that Abram should take her Egyptian maid, Hagar, to be his wife. Abram agreed. It is doubtful whether Hagar agreed. After all, Abram was appallingly old!

I think Sarah must have forced Hagar to marry him,

for we are told that the moment Hagar knew that she would be a mother, she despised Sarah.

A family feud followed, in which Sarah made Hagar's life so unbearable that she fled into the wilderness, to a sacred well, attached to which was probably a sanctuary. It was a holy place and therefore a psychic place.

Here, Hagar seems to have become clairaudient and clairvoyant, for she heard and saw "the angel of the Lord"—Yahweh's messenger.

She must have been astonished to hear him address her as "Hagar, Sarah's handmaid"—he evidently knew all about her—and advised her to return to her mistress and to submit to her.

He told her that her son was to be called Ishmael, i.e., "God-hear," because God had "heard" of her ill-treatment and sufferings. Hagar called the messenger "God-seen" because, as she put it, she had "seen" God.

How human and helpful these stories are! What a wavering and unstable faith Abram's was! Yet "it was counted to him for righteousness."

He certainly distrusted his guide's power to fulfil his promise of a son. He distrusted him, too, when he feared Pharaoh's princes, and weakly allowed Pharoah to make Sarah one of his concubines.

It is really most encouraging to find that the "Father of the Faithful" and the "Friend of God" was as human as we are. How often he must have prayed, as we do, some such prayer as, "Lord, I believe, help thou my unbelief."

Abram, at the age of ninety-nine, was still exercising his gifts of clairaudience and clairvoyance. Yahweh appeared to him, and confirmed the covenant he made with him some while before, and told Sarah, who was ninety, that she and Abram were to have a son. This amused Abram so much that he "fell upon his face and laughed," saying to himself, "Shall a man who is a hundred become a father? Sarah is ninety, and shall she become a mother?"

Yahweh insisted that he was able to do what he said he could do, that Sarah would bear a son, whom she must call "Laughter," or Isaac, to remind Abram how he behaved when his great guide promised him a son.

A little later on, Yahweh appeared again to Abram, by the "Oaks of Mamre," where he had already built an altar for the purpose of spirit-communication.

This time, Abram did not at first recognize Yahweh, for he was one of three spirit-visitants, referred to as "three *men*," whom he saw "as he sat at the door of his tent."

I wonder if Abram had been "sitting" at the door of his tent near the altar. Why not? We can only think in human terms!

Abram must have been a powerful materializing medium, for the three visitants were fully materialized. Abram gave them water and they washed their feet. He invited them to lie down under the Oaks while he got Sarah to prepare a meal for them; and a very hearty meal it was!

After dining, they asked, "Where is your wife, Sarah?"

"Inside the tent there," said Abram.

"Well," said Yahweh, "I will come back to you next spring, when Sarah has her son."

Sarah was listening behind the tent-door, and laughingly said to herself, "Marriage bliss for a worn old creature like me, with an old husband!"

Yahweh read her thoughts and said to Abram, "Why did Sarah laugh?"

Sarah called out from behind the door, "I did not laugh"—for she was afraid.

"You did laugh," answered the guide, adding, "Is anything too hard for Yahweh?"

CHAPTER IV

THE Bible is a continuous record of psychic manifestations, and it is the psychic element which gives point to the stories and is an inherent part of them.

None but students of psychic science can properly understand the Bible and interpret correctly the meaning of its stories, for the stories do but corroborate their own psychic experiences.

For example, the story of Sodom and Gomorrah, which is the next story we shall deal with, tells how Abram walked with his spirit guide Yahweh and two other spirit visitants part of the way to Sodom. These three guides were evidently materialized, for they had recently partaken of a meal with Abram consisting of meat, bread, butter and milk.

Now, such a story is simply incredible to intelligent persons who are as yet unacquainted with the facts of psychic science. Spiritualists, however, know that there are well authenticated cases on record, in our own day, of materialized spirits partaking of food and drink.

Then, again, Spiritualists have no difficulty in believing that the three spirit guides *walked* with Abram, for they knew that in our own day spirit guides walked with Robert J. Lees, who was one of Queen Victoria's mediums.

Lees wrote me a full account of his experiences, and

in his books records how his spirit guides used to materialize in his study, sit down on his chairs, hold round-table conferences with him relative to his literary work, and walk naturally about the room.

Arnold White, the famous journalist, told me how his friend, W. T. Stead, whose body had been drowned with the sinking of the Titanic, came to him in materialized form in his office and described exactly how the collision with the iceberg occurred.

Stead actually materialized small replicas of the Titanic and the iceberg to illustrate what he was saying, and White told me that these replicas were so real that he feared the iceberg might melt and flood his office!

Stead then walked with White out of the office, where they took the lift down to the ground floor and, when no one was about, Stead dematerialized. I asked White why he had not blazoned the news in the Press.

He replied, "Because Doyle is now telling the people all about these things, and he can do it so much better than I."

Well, thanks to Conan Doyle and the noble army of martyrs, such psychic occurrences are common knowledge among Spiritualists and enable them to understand similar occurrences reported throughout the Bible.

If Abram is an unhistorical character, and if the stories about him and Lot and Sodom are entirely legendary—they are still of great interest and value, because they show that the writer was familiar with psychic phenomena and knew his readers were also.

In other words, the writer was a Spiritualist who wrote for Spiritualists a Spiritualistic narrative which he knew they would understand.

He goes on to tell us that, after Abram had walked part of the way with Yahweh and the two other guides, Abram and Yahweh withdrew for a private conversation while the other two went on to Sodom.

Yahweh told Abram that Sodom was almost past redemption and would have to be destroyed. Abram feared for his nephew Lot and his family and begged Yahweh to spare the city.

Yahweh agreed to do so if ten righteous men could be found within it. But none could be found. So the city was destroyed by fire and brimstone.

Lot managed to escape with his wife and two daughters. They were literally dragged out of the city by the two spirit guides!

The next psychic story is recorded in Genesis xx, where we find the righteous Abram again resorting to his old trick of disguising his wife Sarah as his sister, with the result that King Abimelech took her into his harem.

Fortunately, however, the king was clairaudient and, in the night, he heard a spirit voice warning him that Sarah was married to Abram. The king gave heed to the warning and the situation was saved. Where would Sarah have been had not King Abimelech been gifted with the psychic faculty of clairaudience?

Once again we find Abram and Sarah reunited solely as the result of a psychic manifestation.

In Genesis xxi, Sarah presented Abram with the long-expected son, Isaac. Abram commemorated the weaning of Isaac with a feast, at which Sarah was stricken with jealousy of Hagar and her son, and demanded their dismissal.

Abram was very grieved about it and sought the advice of his guide who bade him "hearken unto

Sarah" and promised that Hagar's son should become a nation.

So Abram followed the advice of his guide and gave Hagar bread and a skin-full of water and placed her child upon her shoulder and sent her away. Now, that child would never have been heard of again but for his mother's psychic faculty.

The water was soon spent and poor little Ishmael was dying of thirst. Terrified and in despair, Hagar "cast the child under one of the shrubs. And she went, and sat down a good way off: for she said, Let me not look upon the death of the child."

The child cried out for water and wept. "And God heard the voice of the child," and His messenger—though invisible to Hagar—spoke to her, telling her to have no fear, the child's life would be preserved.

Hagar, being clairaudient, heard these words of the messenger and "God opened her eyes" and she saw water clairvoyantly. Think of her relief! Immediately, she hastened to where the water was and filled the water-skin and gave the child drink. A child's life saved solely by spirit agency and the exercise of psychic gifts!

CHAPTER V

THE next psychic story is of the sacrifice of Isaac, and the only remarkable and outstanding feature in it is the "voice from heaven." Let me explain.

Abram's willingness to offer his child as a sacrifice was by no means unique; such sacrifices were a familiar form of religious worship amongst the neighbours of Israel, especially in extreme distress.

The distressed King of Moab offered his son for a burnt offering. In Israel itself Jephthah offered up his daughter. Ahab, King of Judah, "made his son to pass through the fire." The king, of course, would set the fashion in such matters. So, there was nothing very striking in Abram's willingness to offer up Isaac.

The point of the whole story is this: Abram, in his capacity as a great and chosen leader and teacher, had to be taught that God did not require men to slay their children in His honour; all He required was their willingness to obey His commands. Such new teaching could only come through the one and only source—revelation.

Revelation always depends upon one's capacity to receive it, and that capacity is psychical. Religion is revelation, and were there no such thing as psychic faculty there would be no such thing as revelation or religion.

"The messenger of the Lord called to Abram out of heaven." That is the most striking feature of the story. That is the heart of the story. The writer knew it. He wrote the story because of the messenger and the voice from heaven, and because the revelation given through the voice raised the religion of Israel high above the level of the cults of its neighbours.

The writer does not regard the "voice from heaven" as supernatural. Nor does he regard Abram's clair-audience as miraculous. Both are quite natural to him. They would be natural to the members of the orthodox Churches, if those Churches had not substituted shells for pearls, scaffoldings for buildings, and dogmas, doctrines, and threats for personal spiritual experience.

The ecclesiastical language used by the orthodox

is not the language of the Bible. The terms in which the Biblical writers thought are not the terms in which the orthodox think. And that is our difficulty.

The orthodox would understand that part of the story of the "Sacrifice of Isaac" which is of little or no importance. But the only part that matters, the only part that gives point and meaning to the story—the psychical part—would be a foreign language to them. In reality it is Spiritualists who are orthodox. Heresy and ecclesiasticism go hand in hand!

Bishop Paget once said, "the Feast of St. Michael and All Angels," in the Prayer Book, "is a witness *against* the Church. We have so far forgotten these spiritual helpers as to regard them as we do fairies or nymphs of heathen mythology."

The Bishop of London has recently told us that we are surrounded by angels who are doing *exactly the same* kind of work on earth to-day as they did in Bible days.

But the Bishop has never seriously faced the question, "What kind of work did the angels do in Bible days?" His language is angelic but it has nothing to do with *real* angels; it is churchy, not scriptural.

An angel is not a symbolic image wearing a halo. An angel is a spirit messenger "ordained and appointed to succour and defend us" as the collect for "St. Michael and All Angels" plainly states.

As in Bible days, so in our day angels are seen and heard and spoken to.

If a father, living in London, wished his son to marry one of the maidens in Glasgow, and sent his best friend to that city for the express purpose of finding a suitable wife for his son and bringing her back to London, we should deem him mad.

But if that father was a Spiritualist who had been told by his trusted spirit guide to act in this unconventional way, and if his friend was a Spiritualist who was familiar with spirit guidance, and if the son was in close touch with the unseen, it might make all the difference!

It *does* make all the difference, as the following Spiritualistic narrative shows.

In the twenty-fourth chapter of Genesis, we are told that Abram, who was "well stricken in age," was anxious to see his son suitably and happily married. It was very important that Isaac should marry, because Yahweh had told Abram that his son was to be the father of a great nation.

And, as it takes a worthy wife as well as a worthy husband to produce a "great" nation, it was important that Isaac's wife should be a noble character.

Abram was anxious, too, that his son should not marry a daughter of the Canaanites among whom he was living, but that his wife should be of his own kindred, who were still living in the old home in Haran.

He therefore instructed his chief servant to go to Haran, the town of his brother Nahor, and find a suitable wife for Isaac. The servant felt a little uneasy about it and said to Abram, "Suppose the woman is unwilling to come back with me, shall I have to return and fetch Isaac?"

"On no condition must you do that," said Abram, for he knew that he was nearing his end and needed Isaac with him.

The great Spiritualist then declared his complete trust in his spirit guide, and told his servant that Yahweh, who "took me from my father's home," would take from the same home a wife for Isaac.

So the servant set out for the town of Nahor, with ten

camels laden with presents for the prospective bride and her family.

When he reached the outskirts of the town, he made the camels kneel beside the well where, in the evening, women came to draw water. But he was at a loss to know *how* the spirit guide would lead him to the right woman.

However, he felt quite sure that the guide was with him, so he began to speak to him as if he were speaking to a visible friend at his side.

He addressed him as "Guide of my master Abram," and said, "Here I am at the well, and the women of the town are coming out to draw water. Let it come to pass that the maiden to whom I say, 'Pray lower your pitcher that I may drink,' and who answers, 'Drink, and let me give thy camels drink also,' shall be the appointed wife for Isaac. In this way I shall know that I have chosen the right maiden."

Somewhat similar arrangements are made between the guided and the guides to-day. A clairvoyant will often have a symbolic code. If he asks his guide a mental question, he will be shown a symbol which will convey the answer. His guide will have previously instructed him in the meaning of each symbol.

Well, before Abram's servant had finished speaking to his unseen spirit guide, a beautiful girl appeared at the well with her pitcher on her shoulder. Down she stepped to the fountain, filled her pitcher, and came up.

The servant was charmed with her, and, hoping that she was the chosen one, ran to meet her, saying, "Pray, let me drink a little water from your pitcher."

She at once replied, "Drink, sir, and let me draw water for your camels also."

He gazed at her in silence. He was overawed by the

sense of the unseen. His invisible spirit guide had heard him, had responded to the suggested arrangement, and had caused the maiden to give the exact reply.

We can imagine the servant's natural excitement and spiritual joy. The spiritual world was a reality. His master Abram was right. A wife had been found for Isaac.

The servant gave the girl a gold ring, put two bracelets on her wrists, and asked her who she was and whether he might lodge at her father's house. To his amazement and delight, she told him that she was Rebekah, the daughter of Bethuel, who would be glad to give him hospitality. She was no distant relative, but was actually Isaac's own cousin.

On hearing this, the servant very properly bowed his head and gave thanks to Yahweh for his wonderful guidance.

Rebekah hurried home and told her family what had happened. Her brother, Laban, seeing her wearing a ring and bracelets, ran to greet the man at the well and to bring him to the house.

Then the servant told in detail the story of his mission, of how a spirit guide had led him to Rebekah, and he asked her in marriage for Isaac.

Her family were deeply impressed and replied, in effect, "This is wholly the work of Yahweh, and that is enough. Rebekah has been chosen by heaven to become the wife of your master's son. Take her back with you."

Next morning, they asked Rebekah, "Will you go with this man?"

She replied, "I will."

And soon were seen Bethuel's daughter and her servants riding on camels behind Abram's servant and his men on their way back to the "Father of the Faithful."

When Isaac and Rebekah met they fell in love and were married almost immediately.

What a story! The very centre and heart of it is psychical. Had it not been for Abram's psychic gifts and his servant's faith in spirit guidance, Isaac and Rebekah might never have met, and the great nation of which they are the ancestors might have had no existence.

The Jews owe their origin as a nation wholly and solely to Spiritualism. The Christians owe the origin of their religion wholly and solely to Spiritualism.

To return to Isaac and Rebekah. This happy pair, after being married for twenty years, were faced with the same perplexing difficulty as that experienced by Abram and Sarah.

They were childless and there seemed no hope of the covenant made to Abram being fulfilled through them. So Isaac "entreated Yahweh" with the result that Rebekah presented Isaac with twins.

But, before they were born, they seem to have given Rebekah a good deal of trouble. She therefore "went to enquire of the Lord."

That does not mean that she prayed to God in our conventional way. To "enquire of the Lord" meant to consult the oracle at some sanctuary of Yahweh.

Those who recognized and sought the guidance of Yahweh were familiar with the various means by which communication with him could be established. These means or mediums were called "oracles," whether they were persons, places or things.

Places set apart for communion with Yahweh became naturally charged with psychic power and therefore conducive to communication between the spirit world and this world. Abram knew the value of such consecrated places and so we find him constantly "building an altar unto Yahweh."

So Rebekah "went to enquire of Yahweh" at one of these sanctuaries, and her guide had some very interesting things to say about the coming of the twins.

"Yahweh said unto her:

'In thy womb lie nations twain,
Rival races from their birth.
One the mastery shall gain
The younger o'er the older reign.' "

It is clear from these words that Yahweh knew all about the two boys and their future before they were born into this world.

How many persons to-day, other than Spiritualists, ever dream of consulting their spirit guides as to the future of their children and the best ways of training them for their appointed tasks?

If it be true that God has given His angels, His messengers, charge over us, surely it is only natural to suppose that they will seek to make us aware of their presence, and to win our willing co-operation.

The plain fact is that these messengers *do* seek to contact us and do persuade us to seek communication with them. Spiritualists have realized this truth and have obeyed the injunction "Seek and ye shall find." They have sought and found.

CHAPTER VI

MEDIUMS were no better morally in Bible days than they are to-day. Some to-day are good; others are less good. No human being is morally perfect, and mediums are no exceptions.

Abram was at times guilty of lying and deceit. Peter was at times guilty of lying and cowardice.

Jacob, whose story we are about to tell, was at times guilty of lying and gross deceit.

But Abram, Peter and Jacob were great psychics, great revealers of the spirit world, and deeply religious at heart. And it is transparently clear that God called and used these men. They were His chosen instruments because they possessed psychic gifts. They were not chosen on account of their moral rectitude, though their general characters were obviously far better than their occasional conduct would seem to imply.

But they would have been of no greater service to Mankind than Tom, Dick and Harry had they not possessed psychic gifts enabling them to receive from the spirit world knowledge and instruction which they imparted to their fellows.

Let us now consider the story of Jacob. After cheating his brother Esau of his birthright which gave Jacob a double portion of patrimony, and after telling ingenious falsehoods which secured for him his father's blessing and Esau's hatred, Jacob fled from home to his uncle Laban in Haran.

Had some ill befallen this subtle deceiver while making his escape it would not have seemed an act of injustice on the part of providence. But, as we shall see, providence was far more interested in Jacob's psychic gifts than in his crooked acts.

In the twenty-eighth chapter of Genesis, we find Jacob passing the night at Bethel on his way to Haran. The hill of Bethel is not unlike a huge of flight of steps. Jacob noticed this curious phenomenon, and "he took one of the stones of the place, and put it under his head, and lay down in that place to sleep."

And he dreamed of that flight of steps. Creatures in spiritual bodies were ascending and descending the steps. These creatures were not evil spirits sent to haunt him, or demons to remind him of his wicked behaviour. They were angels, messengers from heaven.

The man who had just lied and cheated is granted a vision of angels and more than that, for we read, "and, behold, the Lord stood beside him." What are we to make of it all?

There has been no repentance on the part of Jacob, and no rebuke is given by Yahweh. Indeed, Yahweh blesses him and confirms the covenant "in thee and in thy seed shall all the families of the earth be blessed. And, behold I am with thee, and will keep thee whithersoever thou goest."

On the face of it, Yahweh seems to be as wicked as Jacob, and much more powerfully so. But when it is remembered that Yahweh had chosen Jacob for the psychic gifts he possessed, and not at all because of his moral character, the fact of the story is transformed.

The psychic faculty is essential to revelation. And the more this faculty is developed the fuller will be the revelation. Obviously the ideal medium would be one in whom the spiritual and the psychical natures were equally developed. But the psychic faculty is the essential one for revelation; and, when that which is revealed is acted upon, a life which may truly be called spiritual emerges.

Unless we understand the absolute necessity of the psychic faculty in revelation we shall never interpret aright the psychic stories of the Bible. Some of our best musicians, artists, architects, sculptors and poets have not led particularly virtuous lives. But they have possessed that indispensable, artistic and imaginative faculty without which no art could be produced. No psychic faculty, no revelation. No artistic sense, no art.

Neither art nor revelation is *conditioned* by morality. Both are helped by it but not conditioned by it. And, as only a comparatively few persons have the psychic faculty developed, the Lord's choice of revealers and seers is limited.

The twelve apostles were chosen for their psychic gifts. This is clear when we remember that one betrayed Him, another denied Him, and "all forsook Him and fled." It was not their moral courage, but their psychic power which conditioned their being chosen by Jesus.

Viewed in this light, Jacob was a fit instrument for the Lord's use. He was not a perfect instrument, but was evidently the best available at the time. So we may continue our psychic story with a better understanding and with increasing sympathy with Yahweh in his extremely difficult task.

When Jacob "awaked out of his sleep, he said, Surely the Lord is in this place; and I knew it not. And he was afraid, and said, How awesome is this place! This is none other but the house of God, and this is the gate of heaven."

No wonder he was afraid and filled with awe. He had fled from the wrath of Esau into the presence of his ever-watchful guide.

His alarms were transmuted into religious awe and he marked the sanctity of the spot by setting up his stone-pillow as a sacred pillar (in those days, a pillar or sacred stone was part of the apparatus of a sanctuary), promising to give a tenth of all he possessed towards the maintenance of this sanctuary which he called Beth-el (God's dwelling).

This does not mean that he had been "converted" by the vision of angels and Yahweh. He was still a self-seeker. He only promised to give a tenth of what Yahweh gave him, on condition that Yahweh gave him food and clothing and a safe return to Canaan. A clever piece of bargaining! We do not, however, read that Jacob kept his part of the bargain.

Arriving at Haran, Jacob met his uncle Laban, who was a more subtle bargain-hunter than he. Jacob fell in love with his daughter Rachel, and promised to serve his uncle seven years if he would then agree to their being married. The crafty old uncle agreed.

At the end of the seven years, Jacob asked for the hand of Rachel, but Laban gave him a feast instead. At the feast Jacob was evidently made the worse for drink and, while still intoxicated, his uncle substituted his elder daughter Leah for Rachel and brought her to Jacob. She was veiled and able to deceive him.

Next morning, Jacob discovered the deception and rebuked his uncle, who merely replied, "It is not the custom in our country to marry the younger daughter before the older. Remain with Leah for a week; then we will let you have Rachel for another seven years' service."

Jacob had to agree, and, at the end of a week specially devoted to Leah, Jacob married Rachel, and paid for her by seven more years' work for Laban.

In the end, however, Jacob outwitted his crafty uncle and fled with Leah and Rachel (who had stolen the family's teraphim, or divining instruments), and his flocks and herds and all his vast possessions.

Laban pursued and overtook him, but Yahweh intervened and told Laban to beware of harming Jacob in any way. Laban was, however, desperately anxious to recover the teraphim, but Rachel was equally anxious that he should not do so. She cleverly concealed them in the saddle of the camel on which she was riding and Laban failed to find them.

Jacob's life was saved by the intervention of Yahweh, who caused Laban to hear his voice. And the interesting point is that Laban would not have invented Yahweh's warning, for it had prevented him from fulfilling his fell purpose, and he frankly told Jacob so in these words:

"It was in my power to do you hurt: but the God of your father spake unto me yesternight, saying, Take heed to thyself that thou speak not to Jacob either good or bad."

Once again, it is the psychic element in the story that is the most important part of it, for we might have heard no more of Jacob had not Yahweh prevented Laban from doing him hurt.

The revelations made to Jacob and the other great mediums of the Old Testament were for the purpose of convincing men that there was another life after "death," that the rulers of earth life were not kings and queens, pharaohs and priests, but Yahweh and his messengers, and that it was at men's peril that they refused to hear the voices that spake from heaven.

That was the primary object and it could not be achieved apart from mediumship. The ultimate object was to reveal to Mankind the true nature of the one God and to teach men to obey Him.

But the important thing was to convince men of the survival of the soul after "death," and it was as difficult a task in those days as it is to-day—presumably much more difficult.

While the Old Testament is full of spirit communications which convinced men of the existence of another and higher life, they did not convince men of the survival of the full personality after "death."

It is one of the most difficult things in the world to convince men, and to make them fully conscious of the fact, that we do survive bodily death. Even to-day the Christian Church cannot believe it.

It teaches that the "dead" are in the graves and will remain there till the "glorious resurrection of the last day," and that only those "in Christ" may cherish the "hope" of resurrection.

A bishop recently consecrated a new burial ground and used these words, "We do now consecrate this ground to be the resting-place of the dead until the glorious resurrection of the last day."

The human mind seems incapable of evolving the thought of universal survival after physical death. This truth has to be revealed and demonstrated, and the revelation and demonstration can only be given through mediums.

And it would seem as if God has ever sought to defend and preserve mediums at the risk of being thought a condoner of their imperfections.

CHAPTER VII

How a slave became a Prime Minister, solely through the exercise of his psychic gifts, is the story we are about to tell. It begins in the thirty-seventh chapter of Genesis.

Jacob had many sons but he specially favoured Joseph, probably because he knew that heaven did too, and gave him a long tunic with sleeves such as only persons of great distinction wore. Joseph's brothers had to content themselves with short, sleeveless tunics, and this made them hate Joseph.

While still in his 'teens, Joseph had two symbolic and prophetic dreams in which his brothers' sheaves of corn were seen to do homage to his sheaf, and the sun, moon and eleven stars made obeisance to him.

These dreams he told to his brothers, who hated him the more; and, having stripped him of his noble tunic, they sold him to some traders who, in turn, sold him to the governor of Pharaoh's prison.

Joseph soon became popular with the governor, who frankly acknowledged that "Yahweh was with him," and that this spirit guide "made all that he did to prosper in his hand."

The governor made him his personal attendant, and then chief warder of the prison. Later, he had in his charge two high officials of the Egyptian court who had offended Pharaoh. They were the Lord High Butler and the Lord High Baker.

These two prisoners each dreamed a dream, which Joseph interpreted. There was no doubt in Joseph's mind as to the correctness of his interpretation. He merely said, "This is the interpretation." His guide had given it him, and everything he told them came to pass.

Pharaoh also dreamed and dreamed again—of fat and lean kine, of full and thin ears of corn. These dreams haunted him. Neither his "magicians" nor the "wise men" could interpret them. Then spake the Lord High Butler, who had been reinstated as Joseph said he would be, "A young Hebrew did interpret truly dreams which I and the Lord High Baker dreamed when in prison."

Pharaoh at once sent for Joseph and asked whether he could interpret his two dreams. "I cannot," said Joseph, "but my guide's interpretation will answer Pharaoh."

Pharaoh then told him his dreams, and Joseph said, "The two dreams have the same meaning. They were doubled because the thing they signify will surely come to pass, and that right soon. God has been showing Pharaoh that there is to be a seven-years' famine in the land."

Pharaoh at once recognized Joseph's amazing psychic powers and deemed him a heaven-sent medium. He trusted him completely.

And when Joseph urged, "Let Pharaoh look out a man discreet and intelligent, and put him in control of the land of Egypt, and appoint food-controllers, and store up food in reserve for the coming famine," Pharaoh answered, "Can we find any one equal to this man in whom is a spirit of God?"

Now, Pharaoh cannot have meant that he was impressed by the goodness and spirituality of Joseph, for neither of these virtues is a sufficient qualification for premiership, and Pharaoh was shrewd enough to know it.

But in Joseph he saw a man who was obviously and

confessedly under direct guidance from the unseen, and he was convinced that Joseph would receive the necessary instruction from his spirit guide.

What psychic gifts or means did Joseph employ in order to obtain spirit messages and guidance? He mentioned one; there were probably others. He must, surely, have been clairvoyant and/or clairaudient, for he foresaw the fate of the baker and butler, and heard his guide's interpretation of their dreams.

We are told, however, that he sometimes used a silver cup as a divining instrument. Joseph told his house steward to hide his silver cup in Benjamin's sack before his brothers returned to Jacob.

The steward was then to send them away, follow them, overtake them, challenge them with stealing the cup, and say, "Why have you stolen the silver cup, the very cup with which my lord *divines?*"

And when his brothers were brought before Joseph, he said, "Know ye not that such a man as I am indeed divine?" The words "such a man as I" imply that in those days to be great was to be a diviner.

Joseph was a Spiritualist and an excellent medium. Pharaoh knew it and for that reason, and that reason alone, said to him, "You shall be Prime Minister."

Like all informed Spiritualists, Joseph knew that we each have our appointed task to perform, that guides are given charge over us, that providence shapes our ends, and that out of evil cometh good.

This is clearly shown in that exquisite part of the story where Joseph makes himself known to his brothers. He bids them "be not grieved, nor angry with yourselves, that ye sold me hither, for *God did send me before you* to preserve you, to save you from starvation by a great deliverance."

Joseph saw the hand of God in everything that had happened to him. His symbolic and prophetic dreams were to him heaven-sent; his brothers' jealousy, his being sold into slavery, his imprisonment—were made by God to serve His purpose.

As he traced the steps of his career, from shepherd to Prime Minister, he realized that he had always been under special guidance from above. His guide had never left him.

Now, most Bible commentators regard Joseph as a classic example of a man of faith. He certainly had a strong faith. But what gave it him? Was it not the *knowledge* he derived from the exercise of his psychic gifts? He did not live "by faith alone." He *knew*.

At the age of seventeen, he dreamed dreams and saw visions. He knew that he had been ordained and appointed to rule, that even his parents were to do him homage. Being sold into slavery was to him a mere incident—albeit an unpleasant one—in his destined career.

His imprisonment was to him more than a mere incident for, in that prison, his guide prepared the way for him to exercise his psychic gifts in the presence of a high official of Pharaoh's court.

Thus did Joseph see that, in spite of his sufferings, God's plan for him was slowly, and in the most unexpected ways, being fulfilled.

Imagine the thoughts at the back of his mind when Joseph said to the butler, who, he knew, had influence at court, "Remember me when you are re-instated, and mention my name to Pharaoh."

No, Joseph did not live "by faith alone." He had his guide behind him, with him, and ahead of him preparing the way—as all men have, did they but know it.

A Prayer Book collect definitely states that our guides are "ordained and appointed" by God to "succour and defend us."

Unfortunately, these guides are called "angels" in the collect, and most orthodox Church folk—including bishops, clergy and ministers—regard angels as celestial beings of an entirely different order from ourselves.

They are sexless. They are never seen. They may be sent to us but must not be sought by us. Their ministry must be unconsciously accepted, but they must forever remain the unrecognized agents of God.

An unorthodox bishop was once bold enough to put the matter thus:

"For years past the Church's injunction for the observance of the Feast of St. Michael and All Angels has been, I fear, rather *a witness against us* than a benefit to us.

"Angels are really no more to us than the fairies or nymphs of heathen mythology. We quietly put them aside with the romance of dim and distant ages, but, at any rate, as altogether out of keeping with our bustling, enquiring, philosophical (but very shallow) times.

"We enshrine their bright forms in our imagination as connected with what has been called the poetry of religion, but to ourselves individually they are nothing."

A perfectly true statement. These celestial, winged creatures of Churchianity have no existence. That is why to Church folk individually "they are nothing."

The heroes of the Old Testament were made courageous, and given faith, by the God who has "ordained and appointed" His messengers, to "succour and defend" us, and to be seen and heard and spoken to by us as they were by them of old time.

As it was in the beginning, is now, and ever shall be.

CHAPTER VIII

A MEDIUM united the clans of Israel.

Strictly speaking, the Israelites were not a nation, but were merely a number of unorganized clans owning the same ancestry, until the great medium—Moses—welded them together into a nation.

The life-story of Moses is too well known to need re-telling in detail. He was born to a couple of the tribe of Levi and was a handsome child. His father was evidently a Spiritualist, for we are told that Yahweh was his guide.

Three months after his birth, the child was exposed among the reeds on the banks of the Nile. An Egyptian princess found him and adopted him. When he grew up he naturally received the best education as a son of Pharaoh's daughter.

He might easily have become a Pharaoh and lived a life of luxury. But Moses was determined to get to know his fellow-countrymen, who were in slavery under Pharaoh and were being "crushed with heavy loads." He saw an Egyptian striking a Hebrew. Moses promptly knocked the Egyptian down so hard that it killed him.

Pharaoh sought to slay Moses for murder, but Moses fled to the land of Midian. There he rested by a well and was met by seven shepherdesses who were seeking water for their father's flock.

Some shepherds came and attempted to drive them away. Moses at once went forward and, proving more than a match single-handed for these bullying shepherds, helped the girls to water their flock. The girls reported this to their father. With him Moses lived for a long time as shepherd and married one of his daughters.

With his shepherd-life began his psychic development and, one day, after leading his flock to the sacred mountain of Horeb, "the angel of the Lord appeared to him in a flame of fire out of a thorn-bush, yet the bush was not consumed."

Spiritualists will find no difficulty in understanding this, for they are familiar with psychic lights which appear as "flames of fire" but do not burn anything. And they know that these flames herald the appearance of messengers from the unseen.

Moses seems to have been a little startled by the "flame of fire" which did not consume the bush. It may have been his first experience of a psychic phenomenon. But he was not terrified by it, nor did he run away crying, "There are devils at work here." He investigated. He "turned aside" to discover why the bush was not burnt. And when his guide—saw that he was sufficiently intelligent and balanced not to fear but to investigate, Yahweh spoke to him in a perfectly natural way, calling him by his name "Moses."

Moses answered equally naturally, "Yes, I am here."

Yahweh then told him not to come any nearer to the bush, but to remove his sandals because he was standing on "holy ground." The place was probably the site of an ancient sanctuary, the psychic atmosphere of which provided helpful conditions for the psychic phenomena known as materialization and the direct voice.

Moses was warned not to come too near, lest his physical presence should interfere with the psychic structures. Such warnings are constantly given to-day to psychic scientists.

Yahweh then told Moses who he was. He assured him that he was his father's guide, the god of Abraham, Isaac and Jacob, the god of the Hebrew people whom Pharaoh had enslaved. This made Moses afraid.

Perhaps he felt a little ashamed at not having left Pharaoh's palace earlier than he did. "He hid his face for he feared to look upon Yahweh." And Yahweh said:

"I have indeed seen the distress of my people in Egypt, I have heard them wailing under their slave-drivers. So come. I will send *you* to Pharaoh that you may bring my people the Israelites out of Egypt."

To Moses such a suggestion seems a little unwise; he go to Pharaoh! But was it not known at Pharaoh's court that he had slain an Egyptian and was an uncaptured murderer?

So he said to Yahweh, "But who am I to go to Pharaoh and bring the Israelites out of Egypt?"

Yahweh answered him, "I will be with you. And here is my proof that I myself have sent you: when you have brought the people out of Egypt, they shall worship God on this very hill."

Not a very satisfying kind of proof! It was certainly too remote for Moses, who naturally needed *present* assurance. However, he told Yahweh that it would be very difficult to persuade the Israelites to accept him as their deliverer, and that, if he said to them "the God of your fathers hath sent me unto you," they would be sure to ask, "What is his name?"

Yahweh, speaking as an ambassador of the one and only God, told him that his name was "I am that I am." This is a descriptive name. It means "I am—(always)

—that which I am (now, and always have been)." It also means "I will be that I will be," that is, "I can become that which I choose to become; I am lord of my own destiny."

And Yahweh counselled him to tell the children of Israel that "I AM" had sent him to them, that he had seen and heard this spirit, who had called him to deliver them from the hands of Pharaoh.

And "they shall harken to thy voice, and thou shalt come, thou and the elders of Israel unto the King of Egypt, and ye shall say unto him, The Lord, the God of the Hebrews, hath met with us; and now let us go, we pray thee, three days' journeying into the wilderness, that we may sacrifice to the Lord our God."

Now, the whole of this must sound nonsensical to those who know nothing of Spiritualism. How can they believe that a man saw a flaming bush that did not burn, that he saw and heard God who instructed him to tell the Israelites what he had seen and heard, and that he and the Hebrew elders were to tell Pharaoh about it?

Tell Pharaoh! What would Pharaoh make of such a fairy tale? The story is surely incredible nonsense to intelligent persons, unless they know something at least of the findings of psychic science.

To Spiritualists, the story is full of interest. They know that the Bible is a Spiritualist book, and that from earliest times men have seen and spoken to God's messengers, the heavenly guides. They know that even Pharaoh would not have thought Moses and the elders mad when they told him that their God had met them.

The ancients were familiar with that which to most moderns is still unknown. There was constant contact between heaven and earth in earlier days. Men to-day have become sophisticated. They have eyes but see not, ears but hear not. There is no open vision. It is a materialistic age.

Revelation can only be given and received in a Spiritualist age. The Bible is full of revelations, because it contains the records of a Spiritualist age, and it needs psychic knowledge to interpret it aright. Without that knowledge, such a story as the one we are considering cannot be understood in any sane way.

If we turn to one of the latest commentaries on the Bible, e.g., *A New Commentary on Holy Scripture*, edited by Bishop Gore and others, and seek an explanation of our story we are given this, "The dialogue between Jehovah and Moses must be pictured, *not as audible externally*, but as giving expression to Moses' *mental* communings with God."

It is a quite impossible picture! No one but a madman communing with himself could have conceived the idea of a murderer returning to the scene of his crime in order to persuade the chief magistrate, who was also a slave-owner, to free his slaves and deprive his country of their sweated labour.

The way in which our biblical commentators ask us to interpret these psychic stories of the Bible is an insult to the intelligence. But what else can they do? They do not possess the key, the psychic key, to these stories.

They tell us that the Bible is an Eastern book, full of poetic imagery, hyperbole and oriental symbolism. They try, by every manner of means, to give naturalistic interpretations to what are really psychic phenomena. Many parts of the Bible are mistranslated simply because the scholars, in ignorance of psychic science, are unable to make any sense out of the original.

For example, the writer of Judges vi. 34, wrote "A

spirit from the Lord *put on* Gideon," i.e., wore Gideon as a garment, clothed himself in Gideon, or, as we should say, "controlled" Gideon.

The scholars translate as follows, "The spirit of the Lord came upon Gideon." That sentence may have a "religious" note in it, but what does it mean? *How* and in what form did the spirit come upon Gideon?

Was the spirit God? What does "come upon" mean? Does a spirit of God himself come upon men to-day? If so, are they aware of it? Or must we regard the words of the verse as an attempt on the part of the narrator to give expression to Gideon's "mental communings" with God?

The truth is that the writer of the verse was a Spiritualist, that he wrote about a Spiritualist, and that this and all other Spiritualist narratives can only be understood and rightly translated by Spiritualists.

CHAPTER IX

MOSES, the nation-maker, was a man of faith and trust. That does not mean he believed that which *men* had taught him about God and had a blind faith in what he had been taught. His faith was not belief at all; it was psychic sense.

He was psychically gifted and his gift enabled him to communicate with, or rather to receive communications from, his spirit guide. That was his "faith." And he put his trust in that which, *through his faith*, he had been taught.

His trust was by no means perfect, as we shall see. He was human. If we are ever to understand our Bibles we must realize the fact that faith—certainly in the early parts of the book—did not mean what the Churches have made it mean.

It meant the psychic sense and the knowledge derived from it. Moses was chosen, not because he had an unswerving belief and trust in God, but because he was a remarkable psychic. This will become clear as we proceed.

Yahweh sought Moses; Moses did not seek Yahweh. The spirit world seeks us before we seek it. But although Moses heard and saw and spoke to his spirit guide he did not accept, without a murmur, everything his guide told him. No, he was a typical psychical researcher. He used his reason and asked questions.

In spite of many assurances from his guide, Moses doubted whether the Israelites would believe him when he told them that he had met the God of Israel, who had promised to deliver them through him. Moses also doubted whether Pharaoh would let the people go.

Yahweh quite understood his doubts and said, "Well do I know that the King of Egypt will not free my people except by force. So I will exert my force and will strike Egypt with all the marvels I intend to work there; after that, he will let my people go."

Moses still objected that the people would neither believe him nor listen to what he had to say.

"What shall I do," he asked, "if the people say, 'The Lord has not appeared unto thee'?"

Moses had in his hand a "rod"—his shepherd's staff. At the request of Yahweh he threw it on the ground, and it became a serpent.

"Take it by the tail," said Yahweh. He did so and it became a rod again in his hand.

"Put your hand in your bosom," said Yahweh. He

did so and when he took it out it was leprous. On putting it back and taking it out again, it became as his other flesh.

Yahweh then assured him that he would be given power to show these "signs" to the people. If they failed to convince them of the reality of his mission, he would be given power to turn water from the Nile into blood.

Moses was still unsatisfied, for he noticed that, although he had been in the presence of his spirit guide, and had been endowed with power to work wonders, he had not been endowed with the gift of eloquence.

So he said to Yahweh, "I am a bad speaker and have no command of words, and being in your presence has not improved matters."

"Who hath made man's mouth? Have not I?" replied Yahweh. "Now, therefore, go and I will be with thy mouth and will teach thee what thou shalt speak."

Moses was too nervous. The task was too big. So he made a polite attempt to decline the commission by saying, "Send whoever you like, but please do not send me."

Yahweh was angry with Moses for his doubts and fears—"the anger of the Lord was kindled against Moses"—but it did not last long. Soon he agreed that Aaron, Moses's brother, should be the spokesman and that Moses should be to him "as God."

Moses was to speak and act under direct inspiration from God, while Aaron was to be a mere mouthpiece. "See," said Yahweh, "I have made thee as a god to Pharaoh, too."

Now, how are we going to account for this promotion of Moses by Yahweh to a pinnacle of solitary grandeur?

It cannot have been a concession to Moses's fear and distrust, nor can it have been a reward for his trust.

How came it that at one moment "the anger of the Lord" was kindled against Moses and at the next moment the Lord raised him to a position high above other men to be "as God" to Aaron and to Pharaoh?

There seems to be only one sufficient explanation. Moses was one of the greatest mediums the world has ever known. The Lord needed him. He was, as it were, indispensable to Yahweh for the great task of delivering the Israelites from the tyranny of Pharaoh.

Yahweh was determined to use him in spite of all his doubts and fears and polite refusals. It was not a question of merit, it was a question of faith, i.e., of psychic faculty.

Moses was "elected" by the Lord, but it was an election to responsibility and obedience, not to salvation. His promotion was due to the greatness of his gift, not to the greatness of his merit.

But could not the Lord have inspired at least one of the vast multitude of the Israelites? Why choose Moses? Surely there must have been many religiously-minded men and women among God's people in Egypt.

There probably were. But being religiously-minded and being psychic are two totally different things.

Only a psychic, a medium, can hear God's messengers speaking in the "direct voice." It is only through a medium that *revelation* can be given. Mental illumination and spiritual rapture are not revelation, and it is always revelation that Mankind most needs. Revelation gives tangible, objective evidence and demonstrable proof.

There was no "medium of communication" other than the great medium—Moses. The *religiously-minded*

Israelites set up gods of their own to worship the moment Moses's back was turned!

To convince a multitude of despairing, downtrodden slaves that the Lord not only wished but was determined to deliver them, and had the power to do so through Moses, nothing less than an external, objective demonstration of that power was needed. In other words, a demonstration by spirit means of psychic phenomena was needed.

This could only be given through a physical medium and such Moses was. That is why the Lord chose Moses. And mediums are chosen and used to-day for the same reason.

Men to-day have had their minds twisted and distorted by the Church and by science. They do not know what to think or believe. Many have given up thinking or believing anything worthy of thought or belief, and in despair are blindly trusting in materialistic power—money, armaments and suchlike.

What is needed is constant demonstration of psychical phenomena to startle them out of despair into belief. Oh, I know I shall be called over the coals for saying that. I shall be told that we cannot make men religious merely be startling them with an exhibition of psychic phenomena. I never said we could.

I said that we could startle them into "belief"—belief that there is really something worth being "religious" about. Men need to see rods turned into serpents and hands suddenly become leprous. Moses needed them, and it took the Lord all his time to convince even Moses!

Having been convinced solely by psychic phenomena, Moses lost no time in fulfilling his commission. He went home, packed up, and with his wife and sons (and, of course, his "rod"), set out for Egypt. Aaron met him in the wilderness and embraced him, and Moses told him all about his meeting with Yahweh.

Moses then gave him a demonstration of the power with which Yahweh had endowed him, and Aaron was convinced of the divine origin of his commission.

So they gathered together the elders of the children of Israel, and Aaron told them all that Yahweh had said to Moses, who then showed them the "signs" of the serpent-rod and the leprous hand.

That convinced the Israelites that Yahweh had indeed seen their affliction and had sent his two servants to deliver them from bondage. No amount of "religious talk" from Aaron would have convinced them. They needed "signs," as Moses needed them, and as men need them to-day.

Moses and Aaron then went to Pharaoh and confronted him with the words, "Thus saith the Lord, the God of Israel: Let my people go into the wilderness that they may hold a feast unto me."

Pharaoh indignantly refused, saying, "Who is the Lord? He is unknown to me."

He regarded the request as an excuse for "a day off." In his anger he gave orders to the slave-drivers and the foremen not to give the people straw for making bricks —"Let them gather the straw for themselves, but see to it that they make the same number of bricks as usual."

The people could not fulfil so great a task, and the slave-drivers thrashed them. The foremen, who were Israelites, upbraided Moses and Aaron.

Moses expostulated with Yahweh and asked him why he had allowed things to be made so much worse for the people instead of delivering them. Yahweh did not reprove Moses. He was quite sympathetic and assured him that something would shortly happen to Pharaoh which would make him not only willing but eager to get rid of them.

CHAPTER X

"THINGS have a habit of going mysteriously right and then mysteriously wrong, and *vice versa*," said a man to me, the other day.

I hastened to point out to him that the word "habit" was a loose and anæmic word to use, and was in no sense descriptive of the workings of spiritual law, and that the word "mysteriously" was a lazy word.

I then told my friend that what he ought to have said was, "Things always work in accordance with law, whether the law be called 'natural law' or 'spiritual law.' "

For example, we are told that God hardened Pharaoh's heart; we are also told that Pharaoh hardened it himself. Which is right? Both. It is two ways of saying the same thing. God hardened Pharaoh's heart in so far as he hardened it himself.

If a man hardens his heart, the result will be as inevitable as results in the natural world—so inevitable that it may be said that God hardens his heart. All's God and all's law.

This has bearing upon the subject we are about to consider—the Ten Plagues.

There was nothing contrary to Nature in these plagues. No miracles were wrought. What men call "miracles" are the workings of—how shall we put it?—undiscovered natural laws which may conveniently be called spiritual laws.

We read that "all the waters of the Nile were turned into blood" when Aaron lifted up his "rod" and smote the waters, and "the magicians of Egypt did in like manner with their enchantments. (I wonder where they obtained the water! There was none in the Nile; it was all blood.)

Now the Nile still turns red when in flood; the red marl from the mountains of Abyssinia stains it to a dark colour which glistens like blood in the light of the setting sun. That is due to the workings of natural law.

But Moses and Aaron arriving at Pharaoh's palace just before the flooding of the Nile was due to the workings of spiritual law, to Moses's *clairaudience* which enabled him to hear Yahweh say, "Get thee unto Pharaoh to-morrow morning," obviously the appointed time.

Who knew exactly when the Nile would rise? None but Yahweh. Was the rising natural or spiritual? It was both; the two are one.

In the thick, evil-smelling, blood-red waters of the Nile, frogs multiplied and "covered the land of Egypt." Mosquitoes infested men's bodies. Stinging flies brought torment and disease.

A cattle-plague killed all the cattle. A skin-disease infected all men. Hailstorms destroyed the harvest. Locusts devoured every green thing. The hot wind — the Khamsin—raised such a storm of sand and such a cloud of dust as to blot out the light of the sun for three days.

In all this there was nothing contrary to Nature. But when we have said that we have said very little.

No one knows the full meaning of "natural law." So far, we have only discovered a few physical laws, a few psychical laws and a few spiritual laws. These laws we find to be quite natural.

Pharaoh's magicians knew how to make the best use of certain physical laws in the performance of their tricks, but they succeeded in imitating two of the plagues only, and were themselves the victims of the others.

The reason why the children of Israel were not victims was that they had knowledge of psychical and spiritual laws which the magicians did not possess.

We are told that when the plague of sand and dust "covered Egypt with a darkness so thick that it could be felt" for three days, "all the children of Israel had light in their dwellings."

This may mean that the darkness was prevented from coming near them by Yahweh's messengers working through psychic agencies. On the other hand, it may mean that the Israelites did not escape the darkness, but being a psychic people their dwellings were illuminated by psychic lights.

The conditions were perfect. The darkness "could be felt." And Spiritualists know that, under such excellent conditions, rooms do often become luminous with psychic light.

To the uninitiated, this may sound sheer nonsense. But to thinkers, students and scientists such as F.W.H. Myers, Sir William Crookes, Sir William Barrett and Sir Oliver Lodge it is common knowledge.

Psychic lights are natural, as natural as gaslight or electric light, but, not being a commercial commodity, they cannot be bought!

In her book, *Ancient Lights*, Mrs. St. Clair Stobart

tells us that the whole episode of the Ten Plagues is a parable, and what she says is so excellently put that I quote it in full:

"Pharaoh represents the sceptical world that over and over again hardens its heart and demands from the psychics ever fresh proofs of the divine mandate: the magicians are our Maskelynes, our physicists, our pseudo-scientists, who can manipulate matter but who cannot see beyond the length of their conjurer's wands or the limits of the four walls of their laboratories, and who deny the possibility of an extension of the scientific world outside the limits of that small portion of the universe with which they are familiar.

"And Moses and Aaron represent the ever-growing band of brave psychic researchers, who, though diffident of their powers, are ready to risk ridicule and the loss of that which is more precious than life itself—scientific reputation—for the sake of delivering the world from the bondage of materialism and guiding it to the promised land.

"And, as of old, the faculties of the heaven-inspired psychics triumphed over the art of the earth-bound sorcerers of Pharaoh's court, so to-day will spiritual truth prevail over materialism, if it is but bravely championed.

"We have no reason to suppose that God is less willing to reveal Himself to twentieth-century mankind than to those who lived in the centuries B.C.; all that is lacking is a Moses who can see the signs and interpret them for us—a Moses who will not only inquire of the Lord, but will have the courage to obey the commands received from the spirit world."

The continuance of the plagues made Pharaoh more and more nervous. He said he would let the people go. Then he refused permission. He kept changing his mind.

He then offered, as a compromise, to allow the people to hold their festival in Egypt, but that if they crossed the frontier they must leave either their children or their flocks in Egypt. Moses was adamant; he stood fast by his demand: "Not a hoof shall be left behind."

Pharaoh was furious, and refused to grant it.

"Begone," he said, "leave my presence and never enter it again. For the day you enter my presence, you die."

Moses answered, "You have spoken a truth. I will never again enter your presence."

And at midnight, "it came to pass that the Lord smote all the firstborn in the land, and there was a loud wail in Egypt; for there was not a house where there was not one dead."

Then Pharaoh and his people implored Moses and Aaron and the children of Israel to leave Egypt at once.

This last plague—the slaying of the firstborn—affords an opportunity for us to consider what is likely to be the best attitude to adopt towards the Bible when seeking to account for such a phenomenon.

The traditionalist has an easy explanation which is no explanation at all. He believes the "slaying of the first-born" is historic fact "because the Bible has reported it," that is "because it is in the Bible."

The Modernist reminds us (a) that the event was not committed to writing until four centuries or more after it occurred, and that the story of it does not represent an exact recollection of actual fact, (b) that physical nature is a closed and uniform system which excludes the possibility of extra-physical happenings.

The Spiritualist could not believe in the "slaying of the firstborn" merely because "the Bible says so." But, knowing that the Bible is a Spiritualist book written by Spiritualists for Spiritualists about Spiritualists, and that Spiritualists to-day are witnessing similar phenomena to those recorded in the Bible, he would attach considerable importance to the reported "slaying of the firstborn" because "the Bible says so."

On the other hand, the Spiritualist, while gratefully acknowledging his debt to higher criticism—of which Modernists make so much—submits that there is a psychical criticism which is far higher than higher criticism. He cannot accept the Modernist view that "physical nature is a closed and uniform system."

His experience confirms the dictum of the *British Medical Journal* that there is no tissue of the human body wholly removed from the influence of spirit. He knows that he can influence or change what is called "nature;" he can move his own body and other bodies.

Lord Kelvin maintained that from the point of view of science every free action was a miracle, that is "no human action is explicable in scientific terms."

The Spiritualists knows that "nature," so-called, is to a great extent plastic to the influences exerted upon it by the free human spirit and to a far, far greater extent plastic to the influences exerted upon it by discarnate human spirits.

The Spiritualist knows that spirit-scientists can dematerialize the human body and other bodies, and do all manner of extraordinary, super-normal and amazingly wonderful things of which the advocates of a "closed and uniform system of nature" know nothing.

Thus, to a Spiritualist, the "slaying of the firstborn" may have taken place. He would not necessarily regard it as an historic fact, but, assuming it to have been *morally* justifiable, he would see no *reason* why it should not have happened.

The Spiritualists attitude is the sanest and the most scientific one to adopt when seeking to understand and interpret the super-normal element in Bible stories.

CHAPTER XI

MOSES was a great physical medium. He was also a remarkable clairvoyant and clairaudient, and he used his God-given powers in the service of God and mankind. That is why he was one of the outstanding men in world history.

The story of Moses can only be appreciated and understood if it is given a psychic interpretation. Otherwise, it is not worth reading, because it does not make sense.

In our last article, we left Pharaoh imploring Moses and the children of Israel to leave his country at once. Then began the most wonderful march in all history, if it be "history." I say, "if it be history," because it is not my purpose in this book to attempt to prove the historical accuracy of these psychic stories, but to show that they are *psychic* stories, whether they be historical or not.

The point is this: given a psychic interpretation, the stories may well be historical, whereas without a psychic interpretation they are utterly incredible, and it is a sheer waste of time to read them.

Moses was faced with an enormous task. He had to direct the march of 600,000 men, with their women and children, out of Egypt. There must have been at least 3,000,000 in all according to the story, and Moses must have spent much time beforehand in planning the exodus.

He marched the men "five in a rank" to the frontier, twenty miles away. The women and children followed in wagons, and vast numbers of flocks and herds choked the roads leading to the wilderness.

Moses did not forget to take with him "the bones of Joseph." Why was that? Because it was around these bones of the old chieftain that Israel's hopes clustered during their 400 years of slavery in Egypt. For had not Joseph "made the Israelites swear an oath, saying, God will surely visit you, and ye must carry my bones away with you"?

Joseph had foreseen that Israel would one day leave Egypt and journey to the Promised Land. It was more than a guess. Joseph was clairvoyant and clairaudient and his prophecy was now fulfilled.

Could there have been any *use* in taking the bones of the old chieftain with them? I wonder. I prefer to wonder than to laugh at such an idea. I wonder how far it is possible for material things to become impregnated with spiritual forces.

I wonder whether it is true that a "dead" man was restored to life by coming into contact with the bones of Elisha. The Bible says so.

I wonder whether St. Paul knew more about these things than we do. He certainly allowed his own handkerchiefs and aprons to be carried to the sick and "diseases departed from them and evil spirits went out."

It is no longer a sign of superior intelligence to laugh at the idea that invisible influences may come from handkerchiefs, aprons and bones. I do not doubt that houses, furniture and clothing are vehicles of invisible influence.

We may yet discover that it is not wise to touch the tombs of Egypt with an unhallowed, archæological hand. And what do we mean when we speak of the interior of sacred buildings as being "charged with power"?

Matter "did not matter" to our great-grandparents, but it matters a great deal to us, because of our changed view of its nature. Physical science has done more than shake us to "atoms." It has shaken us to "whirling electrons." It has shaken the bottom out of matter.

Psychical science has seen into "the soul of the matter" and made us for ever chary about denying the possibility of material things becoming impregnated with spiritual forces.

That great psychic, Joseph, and his successor, Moses, may have known more of this subject than we think. So Moses "took the bones of Joseph with him" and began the march.

Day by day, a "pillar of cloud" led them, and by night a "pillar of fire." What was this "pillar"? Was it something altogether miraculous, something quite supernatural, something that showed itself at that time only and had never before, and has never since, been seen or heard of?

If it were so, it would in no way help us in our understanding of the workings of God. The modern mind cannot believe in a God Who works arbitrary miracles. But the modern mind, instructed in psychic science, can offer a perfectly feasible interpretation of this "pillar."

By day, it was an ectoplasmic cloud which screened off the Israelites from their enemy and also screened off the radiance of Israel's guide, "a mighty angel came clothed with a cloud."

These "psychic clouds" are well known to psychic scientists and are constantly referred to in the Bible, e.g., "The glory of the Lord appeared in the cloud," "The Lord said, Lo, I come unto thee in a thick cloud," "I will appear in the cloud on the mercy seat," "A cloud received him out of their sight."

These are ectoplasmic clouds. The "pillar of fire" was psychic light which is also well known to psychic scientists. None but Spiritualists can understand the Bible!

Guided by the "pillar," Moses and the Israelites marched on and on until they came to the great impassable cliffs of the mountain Baal Zephon. They seemed caught in a trap. On the left hand was the sea, on the right the desert sands, in front the mountain cliffs. What a position!

If by any chance Pharaoh were to change his mind and pursue them, there was no escape except into the Red Sea. Pharaoh did change his mind when he saw the brick-fields deserted and the work at a standstill for want of slaves, and he pursued them.

Picture the scene: the Egyptian horses and chariots show themselves on the desert hills. The Israelites are terror-stricken. They cry out to Moses, "Why have you misguided us? Why did you bring us out of Egypt? Why did you not let us alone that we might continue to serve the Egyptians?"

What wretched creatures these Israelites were! This was but the beginning of a long series of rebellings and cryings and howlings that nearly broke the heart of their great-hearted leader. Moses quickly assured them that all would be well.

"*Fear not,*" *he said.* "*Stand still and watch how the Lord will deliver you; for as surely as you see the Egyptians to-day, you shall never see them again. The Lord will fight for you, and you have only to stand still.*"

How did Moses know all this? Who had told him? He had either heard it from Yahweh, or seen it clairvoyantly or in a vision. It must have been information conveyed psychically in one way or another.

"*The angel of God now moved to the rear between the frightened children of Israel and the Egyptian hosts.*" We may note here that the terms "God," "Lord," "Angel," "Angel of God," "Angel of the Lord" are used indiscriminately for manifesting spirits.

"The pillar of cloud" also removed from before them and stood behind them, thus hiding the movements of Israel. The enemy faced darkness while the Israelites had light which enabled them to prepare for the crossing of the Red Sea.

No miracle happened. Nothing contravened the laws of Nature. Guidance from the spirit world is not miraculous. Clairvoyance and clairaudience are natural spiritual gifts. But what happened was very wonderful.

Moses may have known that a strong east wind blowing all night could make their passage possible. He may himself have escaped at that very spot years before. But no amount of intuition or subtle reasoning could have told Moses the day and the hour when the east wind would blow all night. Yahweh alone knew, and he must have assured Moses that it would happen at the critical moment.

The seemingly miraculous thing was that Yahweh should have known that Pharaoh would pursue Israel at the time when an east wind would temporarily drive back the waters, and that he should have led Israel into what looked like a death-trap and should have told Moses that the seeming death-trap was the gate of life, and that Moses should have been able to hear what Yahweh said.

"*And the Lord caused the sea to go back by a strong east wind, and the waters were divided. And the Israelites went into the midst of the sea upon dry ground. And the Egyptians pursued, and went in after them into the midst of the sea, and the waters returned and covered the chariots and horsemen, even all the host of Pharaoh; there remained not so much as one of them. But the children of Israel walked upon dry land.*"

Well, that is the story which unless it be given a psychic interpretation does not make sense. And no good can come from telling such stories to infants or adults unless we offer them some reasonable explanation. Even our children are being taught to-day to think, to reason and to ask questions.

They will not be put off with mere pious statements, such as "It was miraculous. God can do anything," for they are quick to ask, "Why, then, does not God do such things to-day?" And unless we can assure our children that He does, and tell them much about those wonder-working "gifts of the Spirit," they will continue to prefer to read *modern* fairy tales.

For the Church to allow these stories to be read in public without any attempt being made to comment on them is, in my judgment, sheer folly.

They merely create in the minds of our young people, and of most old people too, the idea that the Bible is too sacred for any one to expect to understand it, and that all it says must be "accepted by faith" and "left at that." The result is that the Bible is "left at that." It is left unopened and unread.

CHAPTER XII

THE Ten Commandments were psychically given to Moses.

The droning of "*God spake these words and said*" in orthodox churches every Sunday conveys exactly nothing to hearers. None but the ignorant believes that the great eternal God the universe spoke to Moses. The words "God spake" are an offence to the intelligence.

But the Churches continue to use them because the Churches are far more interested in "traditional usage" than in either intelligence or truth. And such words as "He gave unto Moses the two tablets of the law *written with the finger of God*" leave Churchfolk confounded and nonplussed, their only hope being to try and believe what they feel to be unbelievable, if not untrue.

Spiritualists, however, are neither confounded nor nonplussed, nor is their faith unduly strained by such words. They find no real difficulty in understanding this psychic story of clairaudience, direct voice and spirit writing.

And they know that the word "God" stands for a spirit communicator who is often Yahweh, the great spirit guide or angel-guide of the children of Israel.

Indeed, we are told that the Ten Commandments were given "through angels," through messengers. Dr. Luke says so in his second book *The Acts*. Paul says so in Galatians. The author of "Hebrews" says so too.

These New Testament writers were not so foolish as to imagine that the Ten Commandments were given and written down by the great God of the universe. They were Spiritualists and knew better.

Oh yes, I know what the higher critics have to say about all this, but I am sure they are wrong. They will always be wrong until they are wise enough to make a thorough study of psychic science. Here for example is the comment made by one of them, Professor Andrews, on what we should call Dr. Luke's Spiritualism:

> "Luke's strong belief in the supernatural led him to exaggerate. Both in the Gospel and the Acts we find an undue prominence given to angelic interventions. For instance, the deliverance of Peter and John from prison is represented as the work of 'an angel of the Lord'; an 'angel' commissions Philip to meet the Ethiopian, and an 'angel' prompts Cornelius to send to Joppa for Simon. The fact that in Chapter viii, verse 29 Luke substitutes 'the Spirit' for 'the angel' of verse 26 seems to show that he does not intend his language to be taken literally."

These higher critics, to whom we owe so much, suffer from a serious complaint known as "spiritual myopia." They cannot see beyond traditional and conventional horizons. Angels are to them a separate creation, "a different group of Beings in the great family of God."

It never seems to have occurred to them that the word "angel" means "messenger," and that "the Spirit" which Luke substitutes for "the angel" is not spelt with a capital "S" in the Greek, and that Luke is merely saying that the angel was a spirit.

He uses the two words interchangeably. One need not be a Spiritualist to know this. It is perfectly obvious to anyone who does not read the New Testament through the coloured and distorting glasses of traditional theology.

The Ten Commandments were given to Moses in the "direct voice" and were then psychically written down by Yahweh on two tablets of stone. These phenomena are quite well known to Spiritualists.

I have myself been present at more than one "meeting for investigation" (that is the real meaning of the word "séance") when spirit communicators have spoken in the "direct voice" and have written messages upon paper or slates without any visible aid.

Let me now tell very briefly the story of the lawgiving at Sinai, and then further comment on it. Israel encamps before the Mount. Moses ascends the Mount to communicate with Yahweh. Yahweh instructs him to tell the people that if they will listen to him and keep his compacts they shall be his own "prized possession" among all nations.

The people promise to do what Yahweh tells them. Moses reports their promise. Yahweh then instructs Moses to tell the people to purify themselves in preparation for his appearance on the third day, and to make arrangements that none shall come near the Mount until the people hear a long blast of a trumpet.

On the third day, there was a "thick cloud" upon the Mount, and Yahweh descended upon it in fire, and spake to Moses out of the "thick darkness." And "when the voice of the trumpet waxed louder and louder, Moses spake, and Yahweh answered him in a voice which all the people heard."

Now then, unless all this be translated into terms of psychic phenomena it is simply double Dutch, double Hebrew, and much more difficult to appreciate than a fairy tale would be.

But once so translated it becomes quite intelligible Spiritualists are familiar with these phenomena. They are the phenomena of the séance room.

The "thick cloud" of ectoplasm was there; the psychic light, "the fire," was there; the "thick darkness" was there; the trumpet was there, and the "voice" of the trumpet was heard.

It is enlightening to know that the trumpet which summoned the people to the Mount was not the same kind of trumpet as that through which the voice was heard. The Hebrew makes that quite clear. The summoning trumpet was a "ram's horn" which Moses had arranged to blow as a signal.

The trumpet through which the voice spoke was quite another kind of trumpet, and we are told it was when Moses was speaking to Yahweh that the voice of this trumpet waxed louder and louder, and the people heard the voice as it pronounced the Ten Commandments. The psychic explanation of all this makes sense of what would otherwise be mere trumpery.

And what of the "thick darkness"? We are told that "Moses drew near unto the thick darkness where Yahweh was." *The Commandments were given in thick darkness by a voice through a trumpet.* What have the anti-Spiritualist orthodox Churches to say to that?

Why do they not hurl their invectives against Moses and Yahweh for countenancing so "dark" a procedure? How can they permit this spirit communication, received in the *dark*, to occupy a prominent place in Church liturgies?"

Why do they not argue here, as they do on all other occasions, that if "darkness" was needed "fraud" must have been present?

Well, whether the Traditionalists or the Modernists

like it or not, the fact remains that Yahweh generally communicated with Moses in a "thick cloud" or in darkness. In this connexion, it is interesting to note that at the completion of Solomon's temple "the priests brought in the ark of the covenant unto its place, into the oracle of the house, the most holy place," which was in thick darkness.

"Then spake Solomon, The Lord hath said that He would dwell in the thick darkness."

A higher critic comments thus: "The dark inner shrine was a suitable place for the Being who had chosen to shroud Himself in thick darkness." What a complete misunderstanding!

Yahweh had not chosen to "shroud" himself in thick darkness. He had chosen thick darkness as the medium through which he could best and easiest "manifest" himself.

After Yahweh had given Moses the Ten Commandments he gave him what is known as "The Book of the Covenant." He then said, "Behold, I send an angel before thee to guard thee as thou goest, and to guide thee to the place I have prepared. Take heed of *him*, for my name is in him, and do all that *I* speak."

Here Yahweh identifies himself with his messenger. "My name is in him" means "he is my ambassador endowed with my authority and power."

The Church believes this, not because she believes in spirit-guides, but because "the Bible says so," and she prays a collect in which she asks that God will send angels to "succour and defend" us, not because she believes in the ministry of angels, but because "the Prayer Book says so."

If the Church had any real belief in angels, in those "ministering spirits" who, as the author of Hebrews assures us, are "sent forth to do us service," she would not so persistently turn a deaf ear to the overwhelming testimony of those to-day who have seen and heard and spoken to God's messengers.

The Church spiritualizes the angels out of existence. Her religion, as distinct from her ethics, is not a real and practical thing: it is something poetical, symbolical and mystical.

The Bible stories are enveloped in a halo of unreality, and any attempt to try and understand them is deemed sacrilegious. We must not inquire, we must not seek to know, for knowledge would jeopardize faith.

But the Bible remains, and the Spiritualist interpreters will yet make it intelligible to the "coming Church" and to the world.

CHAPTER XIII

ISRAEL's spirit guide materialized in the presence of seventy-four persons on Mount Sinai.

"Yahweh said to Moses, Come up unto the Mount, thou and Aaron, Nadab and Abihu, and seventy of the Elders of Israel. And they saw the God of Israel."

Surely none but the ignorant could believe, would believe, or want to believe that these seventy-four persons saw the eternal God of the universe. Whom then did they see? They saw, as I have said, Israel's spirit guide, whose name was Yahweh.

If this is not what is meant by "they saw the God of Israel," the modern mind can attach no meaning whatever to the sentence. For the modern mind, illumined by a knowledge of psychic science, knows, as did a New

Testament writer, that "No man hath seen God at any time."

Indeed, as I have pointed out, the New Testament writers did not believe that the eternal God Himself gave Moses the Ten Commandments. They definitely state that they were given "through angels," through spirit messengers.

Why did Israel's spirit guide show himself to the seventy-four? For the same reason that Jesus materialized in the presence of the five hundred.

Had Jesus appeared to the Apostles only it might not have been sufficiently convincing to His many other followers. Witnesses from among themselves were needed. Both Yahweh and Jesus knew the importance of "many witnesses"; hence the phenomena.

After this materialization séance on the Mount, Moses was again alone with Yahweh, and "the people stood afar off, while Moses drew near to the thick darkness where Yahweh was."

Then followed one of the longest séances in history. For six days nothing happened except the constant appearance of an ectoplasmic cloud. But on the seventh day, Yahweh spoke to Moses in the "direct voice."

The people "afar off" saw bright psychic lights which to-day so often herald the presence of a spirit visitant; so bright were these lights that the people described them as "glowing fire."

Moses had to wait seven days for the manifestation, and the séance lasted six weeks.

Let psychic students who have sat long and received nothing take courage! Some of our best mediums have waited two years and more before receiving any manifestation. But, as they will tell you, and as we know, it was well worth it.

During these six weeks, Moses received instructions for the building of the Tabernacle, its furniture, ritual and priesthood, and as to how the expenses were to be met. The details, as a whole, do not concern us.

We may, however, take note of the Ark, which was to be a portable box of acacia wood inside which the laws were to be placed, and above which Yahweh was to manifest himself to Moses.

Aaron was to wear a garment specially made to hold the oracular stones Urim and Thummim. No one knows what these stones were, but we do know that they were oracles by which Yahweh's will was made known. In the Septuagint version of I Sam. xiv. 41. Saul says:

"O Yahweh, God of Israel, if the iniquity be in me, or in Jonathan my son, give Urim; but if it be in the people, give Thummim."

The Ark was the most sacred object in ancient Israel. It was identified with Yahweh himself, and was more than a symbol of his presence. It was the supreme embodiment of the "presence of Yahweh."

Moses had not been at all satisfied with Yahweh's promise that "his angel" should go before Israel on the march to Canaan; he wanted Yahweh himself.

So Yahweh made a further promise that he would go with them in the shape of "the presence." "My presence shall go with thee." "He brought them out by his presence." "Neither a spirit nor an angel, but his presence delivered them."

Higher than the temporary visibility of his angel, and the transitory "glory" of the cloud, the Ark remained as a permanent possession, the embodiment of, and substitute for, Yahweh's presence.

The Ark, a material thing, was impregnated with the

spirit and power of Yahweh. It could *do* things. Let me give an illustration which may help here and elsewhere. Things are not what they seem; they are what they *mean*.

The upheld hand of a policeman can *do* things because it is more than a hand, it is an "arm of the law." A thing *is* what it *means*. Our king has, as it were, endowed a material thing, the hand, with power to give effect to his will.

The Ark was more than a box. It was endowed with power to give effect to Yahweh's will. And the mere fact that Yahweh constantly manifested himself to Moses "from between the two cherubim which were upon the Ark" would cause the Ark to become saturated and impregnated with psychic power.

It is not surprising, therefore, to find that the "Inner Shrine" which housed the Ark was a sacred séance room called the "Holy of Holies," which was darkened by curtains and screened off from the rest of the building.

Here was the appointed place where the appointed prophets could communicate direct with Yahweh and, in one way or another by the "direct voice," by clairaudience, by automatic writing, by symbols, or by Urim and Thummim receive instruction and guidance for themselves and for the people.

The orthodox Churchman will be dreadfully shocked when he reads the above paragraph. He will regard it as sacrilegious and even blasphemous. I well understand.

The very idea of a séance room being "sacred" must sound to him simply preposterous, because he believes that a séance room is a place where evil spirits capture their prey.

And to call the "Holy of Holies" a sacred séance room is, in his judgment, to come near to committing an unpardonable sin against the Holy Ghost.

Yes, I know this is how he feels about it; I wish I could add, "I know too how he *thinks* about it."

But his feelings are not the result of his thinking, but of his Orthodoxy, of what he has been taught. There was no real thinking behind the cry, "Crucify Him, crucify Him"; it merely gave expression to a form of blood-lust.

How different were the words, "Why, what evil hath he done?"

In this book I am trying to *understand* what is reported to have been said and done by them of old time. I am attempting to think in the only terms in which we can think.

I should like to have been able to think of the "Holy of Holies" as a place not altogether unlike the sanctuaries of our churches to-day, but it so happens that it was entirely unlike those sanctuaries.

And the only terms in which we can think of the "Holy of Holies" are those of a sacred séance room, for that is exactly what it was.

I am not concerned with the historical accuracy of these psychic stories in the Bible; I am only concerned to show that they are *psychic* stories which cannot be interpreted in terms other than those of psychic science.

Moses had a tent and he called it "the tent of meeting." What was this "tent of meeting"? It was not, as one might imagine, a large tent in which meetings were held. It was not a primitive church where men met together to worship God. It was a simple nomad's tent which Moses and Joshua could carry and pitch.

"Now, Moses used to take the tent and to pitch it

outside the camp, some distance from it, and he called it 'the tent of meeting.' And it came to pass that every one who *sought the Lord* went out unto the tent."

Why? Because Moses, their great leader and medium, was there in this sacred séance room.

Yes, the "tent of meeting" was a small but sacred séance room. It was the "house of God" to the people, the house to which men went to meet with God, to tell him about their difficulties and to ask Him questions, and to receive from Him instruction and guidance through His chosen medium Moses. I have said that it was a sacred séance room. There is no other *term* for it. I wish I could have said that it was like the priest's vestry in a church. But it was nothing like a priest's vestry.

No one to-day would dream of going to the priest's vestry, or to the church, or to the Lady Chapel, expecting to find a priest-medium to whom the Lord speaks as He spake unto Moses "face to face, as a man speaketh unto his friend."

If a priest happens to develop mediumistic powers, he dare not use them in the church or even the church hall.

His only hope is to make his own home a "tent of meeting" for his parishioners, a place where all who would "*seek the Lord*" may do so undisturbed by ecclesiastical police.

CHAPTER XIV

THE spirit guide of Moses gave instructions that the work for the Tabernacle should be done by skilled workmen under the direction of two divinely-called and inspired men.

"See, I have called by name Bazelel of the tribe of Judah: and I have filled him with the spirit of God, in wisdom, and in understanding, and in knowledge, and in all manner of workmanship. And I have appointed with him Oholiab."

In those days, even goldsmiths, brass workers, engravers and embroiderers were called and named by Moses's guide.

Moses appears to have written down by automatic writing all the details relative to the building of the Tabernacle, and the Law of the Covenant. These he read to the people, who were in no way surprised at the marvel of it all.

And they were the more ready to believe and obey because they saw that the face of Moses had become transfigured. It was so dazzling to look upon that the people were afraid to come near him.

So Moses wore a veil over his face, to prevent the people from being unduly distressed by continual exposure to its supernormal radiance. But he removed the veil when he went into his tent to speak to, or "sit to," Yahweh, and also when he reported to the people what Yahweh had said to him.

It may seem a little strange to us that the face of Moses should glow and send forth beams of heavenly light. But when we remember that he had spent six weeks on Mount Sinai with his spirit guide, and had fasted all the time, we are not surprised to learn that his face shone.

And if it be said that our mediums to-day seldom show exceptional radiance in their faces, we may well ask how often, if ever, we give our mediums the opportunity of preparing themselves to contact the higher spirit guides, or of remaining for a time in their presence.

Do we not keep them hard at work hour after hour, day after day, week after week, without giving them the opportunity for such preparation? We treat them as machines rather than as the delicate instruments they are, and they give us the best they can, under the circumstances, which is more than we deserve.

Moses found it absolutely essential to guard himself against all influences which might tend to insulate him from contact with his spirit guide. He therefore pitched his tent, or sacred séance room, "afar off" from the people.

It was equally essential that he should guard the people against the debased form of psychism which was prevalent everywhere among the "heathen" nations. Yahweh, and Yahweh alone, was to be their spirit guide. Moses, and Moses alone, was to be their medium and leader.

They were to have nothing whatever to do with promiscuous spirit intercourse. They were never to practise divination, enchantment, sorcery, witchcraft, astrology or any other method of augury. And they must not depart from the strictest adherence to the letter of the law as laid down by Yahweh.

"Augury and divination," says George Adam Smith, "wearied a people's intellect, stunted their enterprise, distorted their conscience."

We must remember that the Israelites had no knowledge of the laws of psychic science such as we have today, nor had they the teaching of Jesus to guide them. They did not know, as Moses did and as we do, that the unseen world is tenanted by those whose influence may be good, bad, or indifferent.

They knew nothing of the injunction, "Try the spirits." And, even if they had known, they were ignorant of the ways and means of doing so. Their only hope was to cleave to Moses and to go to his tent whenever they wished to "seek the Lord."

Even the sons of Aaron were not exempt from obedience to the prescribed rules given to Moses by Yahweh. We read that they "offered strange fire before the Lord, which He had *not* commanded them, and the fire of the Lord consumed them and they died."

They had disobeyed the rules. The fire had not been consecrated, and the sacrifice had not been brought to Moses's tent of meeting. And, however much Moses may have sympathized with Aaron in his bereavement, he was quick to remind him that his sons had broken the sacred rules.

They had probably attempted, by means of unconsecrated fire, to contact other gods or spirits, or perhaps to approach Yahweh himself behind Moses's back.

This rigid observance of the prescribed rules was of the utmost importance to the welfare of these wandering tribes of Israel who, we are told, "went a-whoring after devils and offered sacrifices to them."

Yahweh had said "Thou shalt have none other gods but me." The people had sworn obedience. Yet we find them worshipping devils!

Spirit intercourse was rife among the people whom the Israelites contacted. The "heathen" world took it for granted that communication with intelligent beings in another world was an established fact. But they were ignorant of psychic laws.

So Yahweh gave a most emphatic warning to Israel in these words, "When thou art come into the land which the Lord thy God giveth thee, thou shalt not learn to do after the abominations of those nations.

"There must be none among you who burns his son

or daughter alive, or who practises divination, or soothsaying, no augur, no sorcerer, no one who weaves spells, no self-appointed medium, no magician, no necromancer. Anyone given to these practices is an abomination unto the Lord; indeed, it is on account of these practices that the Lord doth drive out these nations from before you."

And Yahweh adds: "Thou shalt be perfect with the Lord thy God." They were to be perfect in their trust of Yahweh, and were to "love Him with all their heart and with all their soul."

At times he would put their trust and love to the test. "If there arise in the midst of thee a prophet, or a dreamer of dreams, and he give thee a sign or a wonder saying, 'Let us follow other gods,' even if the sign or wonder come to pass which he promised thee, ye must not listen to that prophet or dreamer. It is the Lord thy God testing thee to see whether ye do really love him."

The people naturally wondered what would happen to them when Moses "died." Yahweh assured them that, "the Lord thy God will raise up for you prophet after prophet like unto Moses; unto him ye shall hearken."

In other words, Israel would never be without an appointed prophet, a medium in "holy orders," and the people were to listen unto him as unto Yahweh himself. "I will put my words in his mouth, and he shall speak all that I command him."

Yahweh would severely deal with anyone who disobeyed his commands. "If anyone will not listen to what my prophet says from me, I myself will make him answer for it. But anyone who dares in his presumption to speak a word as from myself which I never bade him utter, or anyone who speaks as from other gods, that man shall die."

The test by which the true prophet was to be known was this, "If the prediction is not fulfilled, then that is a word which the Lord did not utter." If the prophet was supported by events, he was supported by Yahweh. The test was explicitly rejected for the prophets of "other gods."

This makes it transparently clear that psychic communication between good and holy men and good and holy spirits is nowhere forbidden in the Bible; indeed, it is commanded.

A Church which disbelieves in mediumship and has no use for the "gifts of the Spirit"—clairvoyance, clairaudience, automatic writing and the like—is in a sorry plight, for it bases its belief upon the Bible which commends both mediumship and the spiritual gifts.

To those who say, "We believe in Christ, and that is enough; we regard spirit intercourse as dangerous to the living and dishonouring to the dead," I reply:

"No one can believe in Jesus whose does not believe in spirit intercourse, for Jesus believed in it. He spoke to the so-called dead. Angels came and ministered unto Him. He came back from the dead and encouraged his followers to communicate with Him.

"The path of His earthly life is strewn with psychic phenomena. The works that He did were to be done, and were done, by His followers. They were done by the early Church and they only ceased when the Church became unworthy to receive the 'gifts of the spirit.'"

CHAPTER XV

In Michael Angelo's statue of Moses, the prophet's forehead is furrowed deep with wrinkles; it is a care-worn face. The great sculptor had evidently read the words:

"And Moses said unto the Lord, Why hast thou been so hard upon thy servant? Thou art leaving me to bear the burden of all this people. I cannot carry this people single-handed as a nurse carries an infant; the burden is too heavy for me. If this is to be thy treatment of me, pray kill me and be done with it—do me that favour."

Yes, the greatest of all the prophets broke down under the strain of "the burden of all this people," and he reproached his guide Yahweh. The people nearly drove him mad by their distrust and grumblings—" all the Israelites murmured against Moses."

They kept on doing so. Twice they attempted to stone him, and wished to appoint a new leader who would take them back to Egypt. Things came to such a pass that he felt he would rather "die" than continue to endure such suffering in such a thankless task. And he told Yahweh so.

His guide fully understood and sympathised with him, and at once made a very practical proposal: "Bring seventy elders of Israel to your sacred tent (the sacred séance-room) and I will endue them with part of your spirit; they shall share the burden of all this people with you, instead of your having to bear it alone."

So Moses summoned the elders to the door of his tent, and "when the spirit rested upon them they prophesied." How rejoiced Moses must have been at the prospect of having seventy mediums to assist him! But, unfortunately, the seventy were not really psychically gifted, for we read, "They prophesied on this occasion, but did so no more."

Their spiritual wireless sets worked when in contact with the battery of Moses and the sacred tent, but when disconnected they could do nothing. Yahweh had brought them to the sacred tent in order to test their psychic ability, and the experiment did not produce satisfactory results.

Curiously enough, two of the seventy—Eldad and Medad—who had declined the honour of going to the door of the tent, and had remained in the camp, began to prophesy. Joshua seems to have been rather upset about it, and being jealous for his master's honour said to Moses, "My Lord, forbid them."

But Moses answered, "Art thou jealous for my sake? Would that *all* the Lord's people were prophets,"

What a lesson to many of our prophets to-day! The greatest of all prophets knew no jealousy. What he coveted himself he coveted for *all* the people. He would not confine God's gifts to himself or to any limited circle of persons. He was a spiritual democrat.

In contrast to the magnanimity of Moses, we have the petty jealousies of his sister Miriam and his brother Aaron who "spake against Moses and said, 'Hath the Lord spoken to Moses alone? Hath he not also spoken to us?' "

They were jealous of his gifts and unique relationship with Yahweh. That was despicable enough, but they must needs find fault with him for having dared to marry an Ethiopian woman without first asking their consent. I think Miriam was jealous of her; she certainly had to bear the blame.

Yahweh was determined to put a stop to this family feud, so he intervened in order to vindicate Moses's unique position as *his* prophet, and "spake suddenly to Moses and Aaron and Miriam summoning them to come to the tent of meeting."

Yahweh stood at the door of the tent, calling Aaron and Miriam to come forward.

"Hear now my words," he said, "if there be a prophet among you I make myself known to him by visions, I talk to him in dreams. Not so with my servant Moses. I speak to him directly and he sees my very form."

Could anything be clearer?

Moses was a "direct voice" medium, a "materializing" medium, a clairvoyant and a clairaudient. Yahweh made it clear to Aaron and Miriam that Moses, unlike them, was his chosen spokesman, his mouthpiece, "I speak to him mouth to mouth and face to face."

How dared they then speak against the mouthpiece of Yahweh? As punishment for such audacity, Miriam, who was evidently the originator of the mischief, was smitten with leprosy.

The story goes on to show how vastly superior in dignity and power Moses was, for he, and he alone, is recognized as qualified to intercede with Yahweh for the removal of Miriam's disease.

"And Aaron said to Moses, O My Lord, lay not, I pray thee, the penalty of our sin and folly upon us. Let not Miriam be as one dead."

So Moses interceded with Yahweh and said, "Heal her, O Yahweh, I beseech you to heal her."

And Yahweh responded to the earnest appeal of "his servant" and he healed her. Aaron and Miriam had learnt the lesson of their lives.

We now come to the story of the twelve men who

were sent to "spy out the land of Canaan." It is too well known to need re-telling. But a brief glance at the story shows that Moses regards Yahweh as his guide and not as the eternal God. Consequently he does not always agree with Yahweh's judgments, but points out to him where he thinks his judgment is unwise or his memory at fault.

Had Moses thought for one moment that Yahweh was the omnipotent, omnipresent, omniscient God, he would not have dared to question his words. But listen to this: "Yahweh said to Moses, How long will this people despise me? And how long will they not believe in me, for all the signs and wonders which I have wrought among them? I will destroy them with pestilence, and disinherit them, and will make of thee a nation greater and mightier than they."

Moses thought that was a most unwise step to take, and he told Yahweh so in these words:

"If thou destroyest the people, the Egyptians will hear of it, and the nations which have heard the fame of thee will speak saying, Because the Lord was not able to bring this people into the land which he had sworn to give them, therefore he hath slain them in the wilderness."

So Moses suggests a much better course, "Display thy power, I pray thee, but let it be displayed in carrying out thy promise that the Lord is slow to anger, plenteous in mercy, forgiving iniquity and transgression, and who will by no means clear the guilty."

Yahweh sees that Moses's way is the better way, and says to him, "I have pardoned them *according to thy word*."

If Moses had thought that Yahweh was in any sense the one eternal God the story does not make sense. To

Moses Yahweh was a guide, his guide, Israel's guide and, as such, Moses could talk to him as a man speaks to his friend.

Spiritualists do not, any more than Moses did, regard their guides as incapable of making mistakes. They know from experience that their guides are far more superior to them than Moses was to the children of Israel. But they also know that just as Moses was pleased and willing to receive and accept the advice of Jethro the priest, so their guides are pleased and willing to discuss matters freely with them, to receive suggestions, to encourage questions and to answer them.

Guides do not know all there is to know about us. They know a great deal. Like doctors, they have a general knowledge of diagnosis, disease and remedy, but they need our help if they are to diagnose correctly. They are guided best who best help the guides to guide them.

The children of Israel trusted neither Yahweh nor Moses. Signs and wonders, psychic phenomena in abundance failed to melt their icy scepticism. They wanted signs every day, all the way. They were still slaves, not of Egypt, but of fear, doubt and distrust.

The children of earth to-day have made no great advance. They too are slaves. They fear the supernormal. They doubt the facts of psychic science. They distrust the power of the Spirit.

No wonder Jesus said, "If they believe not Moses and the prophets neither will they be persuaded though one rose from the dead."

Those who have blinded and deafened themselves to the spiritual world must not expect to be persuaded, but rather terrified, at the sight of one risen from the "dead"

—if, indeed, they are able to see at all in their blinded condition.

Slowly, very slowly, does Mankind learn the spiritual lessons which this material school of earth is meant to teach. And most of us are still prone to murmur and rebel. But let us not lose heart.

Moses doubted and disobeyed a command, and had to endure remedial punishment. He was not allowed to set foot in the Promised Land. But he still remained Yahweh's spokesman and mouthpiece, his ordained and appointed medium and leader of the people.

CHAPTER XVI

On one occasion, and one occasion only, did Moses disobey his guide.

His sin was great because he was great and his office was great, and greatly had Yahweh trusted him. He seems to have been out of sorts at the time.

He had married an Ethiopian woman, a stranger outside Israel. Perhaps her thoughts and ideals were not as high as his, and this made it difficult for him to keep on the high level.

But his one act of disobedience, coming at the end of innumerable acts of obedience, is a puzzle. Perhaps those wretched Israelites with their rebellings and revilings succeeded at last in lowering the temperature of their great leader's fervour.

Here is the story, a psychic story. The Israelites had reached Kadesh. They ran short of water and, as usual, there was a water-riot accompanied by murmurings of "Why did you make us leave Egypt?"

Moses and Aaron went at once to the sacred séance room and consulted Yahweh, who said to Moses, "Take thy rod, assemble the people, and *speak* unto the rock before their eyes, that it give forth water."

Moses took the rod, assembled the people, but seems to have doubted Yahweh's power to bring water from a rock. So, instead of speaking to the rock, he spoke angrily to the people, "Hear now, ye rebels: *Can* we bring forth water out of a rock?"

Thus did Moses publicly declare his disbelief in Yahweh's promise and power. He then appears to have used the rod—it was Aaron's wonder-working rod—in an attempt to do a little water-divining on his own. The water was there right enough and "came forth abundantly and the people drank, and their cattle."

But Yahweh had told Moses to "*speak* unto the rock," and it would yield water. Moses had disobeyed and, through lack of faith, had robbed Yahweh of the honour due to him.

"And the Lord said unto Moses, Because ye believed not in me, to vindicate my honour before the children of Israel, therefore ye shall not bring this people into the land which I have given them."

Moses realized the gravity of his sin and how necessary it was "for the people's sake" that he should not escape severe punishment. It would show them that Yahweh was no respecter of persons, and would "by no means clear the guilty."

Above all, it would be a salutary warning to the people against disobeying Yahweh's commands. Moses recognized this, and was constantly telling the people that "The Lord was angry with me *for your sakes.*"

We do well to remember that earth-life is school-life,

and that during those forty years in the wilderness Yahweh was educating his people to realize

(1) that they were his chosen people with a leader-medium—Moses.

(2) that, without Yahweh's guidance and instruction and protection, they were helpless.

(3) that they must utterly trust and obey him.

(4) that they must lead pure and holy lives for, "If ye will obey my Voice, ye shall be a peculiar treasure unto me above all people; ye shall be a kingdom of priests, a holy nation."

It was, therefore, a most serious offence for the head prefect in Yahweh's school to distrust and disobey him before all the scholars.

Yahweh taught the people in a very wonderful way, not by instruction only, but by "object-lessons," by supernormal happenings. The psychic phenomena had a definite, didactic purpose. Indeed all such phenomena have, and, unless we regard them as having such, they are worse than useless.

Spiritualism's supreme message is not only or chiefly one of comfort to the bereaved. It is that this world and the spirit-world interpenetrate, and that "death" does not change our characters.

We reap there what we have sown here. The only thing that really matters here is character-building, and the only way to build character is to trust and obey the highest we know.

To return to Moses. "For the people's sake," he was denied the joy of leading them to the Promised Land. He took his punishment like a brave man. Yahweh had told him that he must soon "die" and leave the people he had served so faithfully.

Moses asked Yahweh to appoint a successor, and

Yahweh said, "Take Joshua, a man in whom is the spirit, and lay thy hand upon him, and set him before Eleazer the priest, and before all the community, and give him his commission in their sight."

Moses's spirit guide appointed the man who was to succeed him. He chose Joshua because he was a man "in whom is the spirit," that is, a man who possessed the psychic faculty.

That faculty was essential, but it was necessary that, coupled with it, there should be the qualities of leadership and good character.

And so we find throughout the Book of Joshua that Yahweh is continually *speaking* to Joshua, who heard him clairaudiently or in the direct voice. Joshua was an excellent medium.

Having settled the matter of his successor, Moses assembled "all Israel" and had three long, heart-to-heart talks with them. These three talks are recorded in the Book of Deuteronomy.

They are couched in a strain of eloquent and affectionate admonition, and recall the great deeds of Yahweh in the history of the nation.

Moses reminded them that the Commandments were written "by the finger of Yahweh"—a statement which only psychic students can understand.

He recalled how "The Lord spake unto you, ye heard his voice but saw not his form." The people had not seen Yahweh in a materialized form, but they had heard his voice as it spake "through the trumpet from the Mount."

And the reason why they were not permitted to see his form was this: "Lest ye corrupt yourselves by making a graven image in the form or in the form of any figure."

Moses had had a heart-breaking clairvoyant vision which showed him that the people he loved so dearly would not possess the Promised Land for long. They would again do evil and rebel against Yahweh, serving other gods.

He implored them to remember that "it is not because of thy righteousness or uprightness that thou dost go to possess the land: but for the vice of these nations the Lord is driving them out before thee. Ye are a stiff-necked people. Ye have been rebellious from the day I knew you."

And he made his last pathetic appeal to them. "Ask the days of old, which were before ye were born"—he was addressing the new generation of Israelites—"ask if anything as great has ever happened, or been heard of, from one end of the earth to another: Did any nation ever hear the voice of a god speaking, as thou hast heard?

"Has any god"—that is, a guide—"ever ventured to go and take a nation for himself out of another nation by a series of tests"—he was referring to the Ten Plagues—"and by signs and wonders? Unto thee, and thee alone, were these things shown to teach thee that the Lord he is God.

"Out of heaven he made thee to hear his voice, that he might instruct thee: and upon earth he made thee to see his great fire"—great psychic light—"and thou heardest his words out of the midst of the fire.

"The Lord suffered thee to hunger and fed thee with manna, that he might make thee to know that man doth not live by bread alone but by every utterance that cometh from the mouth of the Lord."

Moses then reminded them of another amazing psychic phenomenon. "Thy raiment waxed not old upon thee, neither did thy shoes wax old upon thy feet, nor thy feet swell, these forty years." The clothes grew with the children who wore them, as the shell grows with the snail.

I am not concerned with the historical accuracy of any of these stories in the Bible. I am only concerned to show that they are psychic stories, and that if any of them are historical they can only be understood and appreciated by those who have a knowledge of psychic science.

Moses then recalled to their minds his faithfulness to them on the Mount, how for their sakes he fasted, on two occasions, for six weeks in order to prepare himself physically, mentally, and spiritually to see and hear Yahweh and to receive from him guidance and instruction.

He told them that he "fell down before the Lord," which evidently means that he fell into a state of trance in which he was able to receive injunctions and messages.

He warned them against false mediums and dreamers who "go after other gods," and condemned the fire-ordeal of Moloch-worship and the eight varieties of pagan sorcery.

But Moses commanded the people to hearken unto their own authorized medium, unto "the prophet from the midst of thee"—not foreign magicians—"like unto me, whom the Lord will raise up unto thee."

CHAPTER XVII

On the last birthday of his life, that grand old medium, Moses, assembled the Israelites and bade them "be strong and of a good courage, fear not, for Yahweh doth go with thee; he will not forsake thee nor fail thee."

He then called Joshua and said the same thing to him, and ordered that the Law should be read before the people once every seven years, that "they may learn to love the Lord, to obey his voice, and to cleave unto him alway."

Yahweh then said to Moses (whose clairaudience after 120 years of earth-life was as good as ever), "Call Joshua and present yourselves at the tent of meeting"—that is the sacred séance room—"that I may give him a charge."

This done, Yahweh sorrowfully spoke thus to Moses, "After thy death the people will forsake me for the foreign gods of the people among whom they are going to live. Write thou a song and teach it to the people that it may testify before them as a witness."

So Moses wrote his inspired "swan-song" in which the goodness of Yahweh was reviewed, the ingratitude and punishment of Israel foreseen, and Yahweh's purpose to intervene and save Israel declared.

Still strong, with "his eye undimmed and his natural force unabated," Moses bade farewell to his people, climbed to the top of Pisgah, saw the Promised Land, and, journeying on to the cloud-capped summit of the Mount, "died" there "according to the word of the Lord."

The Hebrew for "word" here is "*mouth*," which a Jewish commentator beautifully interprets as "Yahweh's kiss."

So Moses, after receiving the divine kiss of approval, was received by Yahweh into the glory of high heaven. A redactor tells us that "Moses was buried in a ravine on the Mount," but adds, "no man knoweth of his sepulchre."

It is hardly likely that Moses buried himself. It seems certain that no human being buried him. It is probable that he, like Enoch and Elijah, was translated to the spirit world.

This suggestion may sound absurd to those who know nothing of Spiritualism, but to the student of psychic science such a suggestion will not seem impossible.

But Moses did not "die," even if his body was in some mysterious way buried.

He came back from the "dead" to let men know that he had never "died." He talked with Jesus on the Mount of Transfiguration and urged Him to "go through with His death at Jerusalem." He had, of course, known all about it. For centuries, he had been one of the leading elders in the heavens.

Common-sense is quite inadequate when seeking to interpret these psychic stories in the Bible. Common-sense cannot make sense of these stories. Uncommon-sense is what is needed, the uncommon-sense of those to whom the super-normal is as natural as the normal.

We are not yet able to write an account of the life of Moses in the spirit world, but, at any moment now, we may be able to do so.

As, through the hand of Geraldine Cummins, an unseen messenger has written for us *The Scripts of Cleophas*, who knows but that an unseen messenger may yet write through her, or through one similarly gifted, *The Life Of Moses In The Spirit World*?

Our next psychic story is one of unusual interest. It is the story of Balaam and the Ass.

Balak, King of Moab, was terrified because the armies of Israel had conquered two other kings nearby, and were approaching the borders of Moab.

So he sent his chiefs to a mysterious magician and seer "in the mountains of the East"—one Balaam—to persuade him to go to Moab and "curse the people of Israel, for I know that he whom Balaam cursest is cursed, and he whom he blessest is blessed."

Balaam was a medium of great fame and reputation. He was no mere magician. He was a prophet of God outside the Hebrew race. He was not one of "the chosen people."

This shows that God's prophets were not confined to Israel, though He was giving Israel special training through her own prophets. Melchizedek, priest of Salem, was not of Israel; yet he "blessed" Abram. We shall see later what "blessing" and "cursing" really mean.

God did not neglect the rest of the world for Israel. His prophets were at work among the other peoples of the world. We must remember that the earlier religions of China, India, etc., were full of high and noble teaching which later became corrupted, just as original Christianity became corrupted by Churchism.

What was it that made Balak believe that "he whom Balaam cursest is cursed"? Was it mere superstition? Or had Balak good reason for his belief?

Balaam was not a priest. He was a remarkable medium, and Balak knew it. He knew that Balaam could see what others could not see, and hear what others could not hear. He knew that he was in constant contact with the world of spirits and could "get to know things."

What do the "cursings" and "blessings" in the Old Testament mean? Were they simply ineffective invocations of evil or good upon an enemy or friend?

They were nothing of the kind. They were predictions made after the exercise of the gifts of clairvoyance and clairaudience. That is why they "came to pass."

The genuine prophets either "saw into the future" or were told clairaudiently what the future held in store. They could therefore guide nations and were worthy to be called "statesmen."

Balak knew perfectly well that Balaam was a first-class professional medium, possessing clairvoyant and clairaudient gifts. So the messengers who were sent to fetch Balaam went "with the medium's fee in their hand" or, as the Bible puts it, "with the rewards of divination in their hand."

We are not told what the fee was. We are, however, told that Samuel received a fee of "a piece of silver," worth intrinsically about eightpence of our money, for the information he gave Saul about his lost asses.

No one thinks any the less of Samuel for having accepted a fee for the exercise of his valuable gift, and we must not think less of Balaam who did the same. "The labourer is worthy of his hire"—providing that his eyes are on his work, not the hire.

Balaam and Samuel needed their fees. Their lives were not miraculously sustained. And our mediums to-day still need fees for food, clothing and shelter.

Well, Balaam refused to accompany the messengers back to Balak—"The Lord refuseth to give me leave to go with you." Balaam seems to have half-hoped that the Lord would let him go. The words "refuseth to give me leave" suggest that he wanted to go and to receive the rewards of divination, but dared not.

Balak was bitterly disappointed and offered Balaam a much larger fee if only he would come to him. This dazzling bribe—"I will promote thee unto great honour, and give thee whatsoever thou askest"—lured Balaam away from the straight path.

He knew that the Lord had already said, "No, you must not go," but he would not take "No" for an answer. He would ask the Lord again, hoping He would change His mind.

Balaam then told the messengers that the Lord had said "Yes." He had been playing tricks with his conscience.

Now, Balaam was riding upon an ass, and "The ass saw the angel of the Lord standing in the way." How very natural! Animals can often see what we humans cannot. And, in this case, we can well believe that Balaam's clairvoyance had become temporarily inoperative—his eyes were fixed on the dazzling "rewards."

The ass turned aside and Balaam smote her. The angel appeared again, and the ass backed into a wall and crushed Balaam's foot, and he smote her again.

The angel "went further, and stood in a narrow place where was no way to turn either to the right hand or to the left, and the ass lay down under Balaam: and Balaam's anger was kindled, and he smote her with his staff."

The story goes on to say: "The Lord opened the mouth of the ass, and she said unto Balaam, What have I done unto thee, that thou hast smitten me these three times?"

This is very interesting to psychic students on account of what follows. Balaam then saw the angel, who said to him exactly what the ass had said to him.

It is obvious that the angel was the speaker in both cases; first, from between Balaam and the ass, giving Balaam the impression that the voice came from the ass's mouth, then in front of Balaam and in full vision for "The Lord had opened the eyes of Balaam and he saw the angel."

Balaam bowed his head and fell on his face and said, "I have sinned, I will get me back again." But the angel told him that he had better go with the messengers now; "but only the word that I shall speak unto thee, that thou shalt speak."

Once again we may note that the terms "God," "Lord," "angel," "angel of the Lord" were constantly made to stand for one and the same spirit.

CHAPTER XVIII

One of the most courageous mediums in history was Balaam. He was grossly misjudged. An infamous and revolting story was told about him. It was untrue. But Jewish and Christian writers judged his character by that untrue story and condemned him as a wicked, grasping seer.

What was the infamous story? Who told it?

The story was this: Balaam, having found it impossible to persuade his guide to give him permission to curse Israel, slammed the psychic door of communication in his guide's face and took matters into his own hands.

King Balak had taunted him with the words, "The Lord hath prevented thee from earning thy 'fee' and gaining high position." So Balaam, being determined to obtain Balak's "rewards," and having failed to do so by fair means, sought foul means.

He suggested to Balak that the best way to bring a curse upon the sons of Israel was to encourage the women of Midian to seduce them by enticing them to commit immoral acts.

The plot met with enormous success, and no less than 24,000 sons of Israel were destroyed.

Who conceived and concocted this untrue and revolting story? The priests.

When? Years after Balaam's "death."

Why? For at least two reasons.

(1) Because their bigotry and exclusiveness would not allow them to believe that Balaam, who was a foreigner "outside Israel," could possibly have been a suitable recipient of a revelation from the God of Israel.

(2) Because their general dislike of prophets made it easy and desirable to bear false witness against Balaam.

If my readers will glance at pages 138-9 of *A New Commentary On Holy Scripture*, they will see how the prophet was misjudged. Here is what the priests wrote about Balaam:

"These (the women of Midian) caused the sons of Israel, *through the counsel of Balaam*, to commit trespass against the Lord."

And this "false witness" caused the author of the Book of Revelation to write: "There are they that hold the teaching of Balaam, who taught Balak to cast a stumbling-block before the sons of Israel, and to commit fornication."

Thus has it ever been, and is even so to-day. The

priests and the prophets have two very different conceptions of religion. Priests to-day delight in telling their people that most mediums are dishonest, that the exercise of mediumship is strictly forbidden in the Bible, that such exercise leads to the moral degradation of the medium.

And the priest delights in telling his people that lunatic asylums are full of mediums and their victims. The fact that it is not true does not interest him, so long as it causes his people to be terrified at the very mention of mediums, séances, Spiritualists and Spiritualism.

Priests know perfectly well that prophets are their inveterate enemies in that they encourage men, women and children to seek instruction and guidance from their guides. Once a person knows his guides, priestcraft loses all its power over him.

Now watch Balaam—that great and courageous medium—at work. As soon as he met Balak, he told him quite plainly that he had not come to curse Israel but to inform him that Israel was the people of God, His "chosen people" who were under His immediate protection. Recall Balaam's wonderful words to Balak:

> "Wherewithal shall I come before the Lord,
> And bow myself before the High God?
> Shall I come before Him with burnt-offerings,
> With calves of a year old?
> Will the Lord be pleased with thousands of rams,
> Or with ten thousands of rivers of oil?
> He hath shewed thee, O man, what is good;
> And what does the Lord require of thee,
> But to do justly, and love mercy,
> And walk humbly with thy God."

Balak imagined that Balaam's God could be persuaded to permit Balaam to curse Israel if only he would offer sacrifices. To correct this erroneous view, Balaam did offer sacrifices, but he said to Balak, "Only the words which God putteth in my mouth will I speak; only what the Lord sheweth me will I tell thee."

When Balak offered to promote him "unto very great honour" and give him any fee he liked to ask, Balaam answered, "If Balak would give me his house full of silver and gold, I cannot go beyond the word of the Lord, to do less or more."

A great and dignified utterance by a noble and courageous medium!

Three times did Balaam, after offering sacrifices, consult his guide. Three times was he told by his guide to pour forth blessings instead of curses upon Israel. And he did so. On the third occasion he was in a trance, with his physical eyes closed, when he heard his God speak to him, and saw a vision of the Almighty.

It was a purely psychical experience. The word "God" can only mean "guide," and the word "Almighty" cannot mean the One Eternal God of the universe, for "no man hath seen God at any time."

What is meant is that Balaam heard his guide speak to him, and he realized the power of that guide's righteousness.

A modern commentator explains this psychical experience thus:—Balaam heard, with his inward ear, God speak, and saw, with his inward eye, a vision of the Almighty.

It will not do. It does not make sense. But it is the only interpretation a non-Spiritualist can give.

Balaam went to Balak and told him that, in trance, he had heard the Lord speak to him and had been granted a vision of the mightiness of righteousness, and had seen the power and the might of Israel who, being divinely protected, would conquer all enemies.

On hearing this, "Balak's anger blazed out against Balaam; and he struck his hands together in contempt, and said to him, 'I summoned thee to curse my foes, and here thou hast blessed them these three times. Therefore, get thee gone, flee to thy house. I had intended to pay thee richly, but the Lord hath prevented thee from receiving the rewards.' "

Balaam answered, "I will return to my home but, ere I depart, I will tell to thee what the people of God will do to thy people in the days to come."

He then told Balak what he had clairvoyantly seen:

> "I have seen Israel in the far future:
> I have marked him in the days to come:
> I have seen a star coming forth out of Jacob
> And a sceptre arise out of Israel
> Which breaks the heads of the Moabites
> The skulls of the creatures of pride;
> Edom becomes the prey of Israel,
> Seir is conquered,
> As Israel wins the day
> And tramples on all his foes."

And Balaam withdrew himself from the presence of Balak.

That briefly is the story of Balaam, and, had it been left at that, what a wonderful inspiration the name of Balaam would have been to us all.

But no one's reputation is safe in the hands of the priests! It is true that he made a great slip, but it was only a slip; it was not a permanent fall. The moment his guide brought him to his senses he repented, and wanted to undo what he had done.

Moses fell, but it was no permanent fall. Who has not fallen at some time or other?

And so we leave this splendid fellow, this "foreigner," this great and good and courageous prophet of God, who was "outside Israel" and outside the sphere of "covenanted grace" as the priests would have said, but not outside the sphere of direct inspiration and revelation.

We leave him reinstated at last, at long last, rescued after many centuries from the wicked and cruel hands and libellous tongues of the priests.

He now stands before Mankind as one of the noblest examples of conscientiousness, unflinching courage and utter devotion to the truth and righteousness revealed to him by his guide.

The story of Balaam is a psychic story from beginning to end. It is saturated with psychic experiences—clairvoyance, clairaudience, trance and direct voice—but it is unintelligible to those who are ignorant of the findings of psychic science.

CHAPTER XIX

ANTI-SPIRITUALISTS assert that Spiritualism is forbidden in the Bible. They base their assertion on certain verses in the Old Testament, chiefly on verses 10 and 11 of the eighteenth chapter of the Book of Deuteronomy.

Those verses read: "There shall not be found among you any one that maketh his son or his daughter to pass through fire, or that useth divination, or an observer of times, or an enchanter, or a witch, or a charmer, or a consulter with familiar spirits, or a wizard or a necromancer. For whosoever doeth these things is an abomination unto the Lord."

These verses no more refer to the practices of modern Spiritualism than the words "Moab is my wash pot: over Edom will I cast out my shoe" refer to modern spring-cleaning.

Spiritualism knows nothing of a fire-ordeal. It knows nothing of Deuteronomic "divination," which had to do with arrows, livers and the like, as, for example: "The king of Babylon stood at the parting of the way to use divination: he shook the arrows to and fro, and inspected a beast's liver."

It knows nothing of the Deuteronomic "observer of times, enchanter, witch, charmer, consulter, wizard or necromancer."

But supposing we were to try and make the terms "consulter with familiar spirits, wizard, and necromancer" mean one who talks with the "dead," how would it affect matters?

Well, it would at once make Jesus "an abomination unto the Lord," for He talked to the "dead"—to Moses and Elijah. He saw and heard and spoke to them. *He spoke, mark you, to the very man who had forbidden such communication.*

Therefore, Jesus either abrogated the law of Moses, or He sinned. In reality He did neither, for, as I have said, the Deuteronomic prohibitions have nothing in common with the Spiritualism of Jesus or with the Spiritualism of to-day.

However, let us try and imagine that the practices referred to in Deuteronomy are those of modern Spiritualism, and are binding on us to-day. If that be so, then the other Deuteronomic injunctions are also binding on us to-day. Let us see how it would all work out.

We will suppose that we are at war and have captured one of the enemy cities. Each of our soldiers, and presumably sailors and airmen too, who happens to see among the captives a beautiful woman, whom he desires to marry, may take her home.

He must then shave her head and pare her nails. If after marriage, he finds that he has "no delight in her," he may turn her out of his house!

We may therefore visualize innumerable bald-headed women with pared finger-nails parading our streets!

And what is to be done with the bad boys of the family? The injunction reads: "If a man have a stubborn and rebellious son who will not obey his father or mother, who will not listen to them even when they chastize him, then the parents shall bring him before the Elders"—telling them what a bad fellow he is. "Whereupon all his fellow-citizens shall stone him to death."

The Bad Boy of Peckham must be brought before the town councillors of Peckham, and the people of Peckham must stone him to "death." These petrifying massacres would be constantly taking place in every city, town and village in the land!

But what kind of clothing would these stone-throwers have to wear? Deuteronomy forbids us to wear "a garment of two kinds of stuff mingled together."

So our coats, jackets, waistcoats, vests—not to mention other cosy articles—would have to be dispensed with. And the newly made one-stuff garments would have to have "tassels on the four corners."

"If a man have two wives," begins another injunction. But that is, of course, a trifling matter. Solomon had

"700 princesses and 300 concubines, and he took foreign wives." Any man was allowed to have as many wives and concubines as he could afford to maintain.

But what about this: "When a man taketh a new wife, he shall not go on active service, nor shall he be called upon to do any kind of business: he shall be free at home for one year, and cheer his wife"?

What a boon to the priests! Think of the enormous increase in marriages and fees. I have a serious purpose in all this fun.

Another injunction reads: "When two brothers live under the same roof and one dies leaving no son, the dead man's wife must marry her husband's brother."

But, supposing the brother does not love, or even like, the widow, and refuses to marry her, what then? She must bring him before the town councillors and "spit in his face." Well, we really cannot pursue the matter any further; it is getting far too unpleasant.

We have said enough to show what life would be like if we obeyed all the Deuteronomic injunctions.

We do not "pass our sons and daughters though fire," nor do we capture beautiful women, shave their heads, marry them, and cast them off in a bald-headed way.

We do not use "divination," nor do we stone to "death" the bad boys of the family. We are not "observers of times," nor do we wear one-stuff garments with tassels. We are not "enchanters," nor do we have two wives.

There are no "witches and wizards" to torment women—perhaps that is why a newly-married man does not stay at home for a year to cheer up his wife. We do not "consult with familiar spirits," nor do we become familiar with our brother's widow.

The best way to deal with Deuteronomic anti-Spiritualists is to "laugh them out of court." It is useless to try and reason with them. They do not reason. Their minds are in the grip of the hydra-headed monster of tradition, ignorance and prejudice.

There is only one way of slaying that monster; we must "*tickle it to death.*" We must make it "*split its sides*" with laughter.

A religious woman went to purchase a Bible. The shop-assistant set before her copies of the Authorized Version, the Revised Version, Dr. Ferrar's *Bible in Modern English* and Dr. Moffatt's *The Bible*: *A New Translation*, and politely asked, "Which version, madam, do you require?"

The woman replied heatedly, "*I don't want any of your versions. I want the Bible as God gave it to us.*"

Now, "tickling" is the only cure for such a disease as that!

An anti-Spiritualist once said to me, "I am sure you do not know your Bible. How many times have you read it right through? I have done so each year for ten years. Why don't you read it? You believe it is God's Word, don't you? You believe it's inspired?"

Such persons usually ask two or three questions at the same time in the hope of making it more difficult for one to answer!

However, I assured the lady that I did not read my Bible from cover to cover every year, as my time was too fully occupied in *studying* the book. But I told her that my favourite Old Testament writing was "The Book of the Prophet Hezekiah." She too delighted in his writings and confessed that she was simply entranced by the beauties of his book.

So I asked her if she remembered the famous passage

in which cricket is referred to as a game played by the Jewish boys. She did not.

I handed her my Bible and asked her to turn to Chapter V and read verse 7. She could find neither the book nor the chapter, though she turned the pages over again and again.

Then, when she thought I was not looking, she hurriedly glanced at the index and exclaimed, "*Your* Bible is not complete; it does not contain 'Hezekiah.' "

"No, dear lady," said I, "there is no such prophet."

She was "tickled to death" and said, "You know your Bible better than I do."

When I was at college, Sir Oliver Lodge was asked by the students to deliver a lecture on "Immortality."

The meeting was open to the public and the public came. One religious-looking woman, however, stood outside the entrance trying to dissuade people from going in by calling out, "It's Spiritualism!"

A student friend of mine attempted to rebuke her, and she said to him, "But isn't Lodge the man who believes in spirits?"

"Yes," said the student, "and he has brought with him a number of spirits which he has preserved in bottles, and he intends to let them out at the meeting for the people to inspect."

The woman "split her sides with laughing" and became quite friendly. The "side" attack had won. She attended the meeting.

I rather suspect that the man who wrote the proverb, "Answer a fool according to his folly" must have had a good deal to do with that type of mind which belongs to-day to the anti-Spiritualists.

CHAPTER XX

We are trying to understand the Bible. We are seeking to make sense of such expressions as: "God spake," "The Lord said," "The angel appeared," "The angel stood" and the like.

Throughout the Book of Joshua, we are constantly told that "The Lord spake unto Joshua." We are also told that "The Captain of the host of the Lord" spake to Joshua.

What do such words mean? Our biblical scholars find no difficulty in explaining them. They just "explain them away" by saying, "What Joshua saw with the eye of faith is recorded as an objective reality. The divine communication was made to the inward eye and ear of Joshua's soul."

But that kind of explanation will not do. It does not make sense. It only makes sensible persons deem it a sheer waste of time to read the Bible.

Dr. Scott Lidgett bemoans the fact that "the Bible is a dead book to the multitudes." What has killed it? Two things, the unintelligent bibliolatry of past generations and the unintelligent interpretations of to-day's scholars.

What can bring it to life again? One thing and one thing only, namely the revealing and revivifying light thrown upon it by Spiritualism. It makes the Bible a living book of extraordinary interest.

Moses was succeeded by his lieutenant—Joshua—in the leadership of Israel. Joshua was told by his guide to lead the Israelites across Jordan which was at that time in "high flood." The task seemed quite impossible.

His faithful guide assured him that "When ye are come to the brink of the waters of Jordan, the waters shall be cut off."

Scholars tell us that there is no reason to suppose that anything supernatural occurred. Of course not. Nothing ever occurs that is supernatural. It is probable that the waters were cut off by a great landslide falling into a narrow gorge of the river.

An Arabic chronicler informs us that in the year A.D. 1267 there was a sudden damming of the Jordan by a landslide, but he does not say that a spirit-guide had previously told someone when the damming would take place!

The point in our story is that Joshua, being an excellent clairaudient, heard his guide tell him that the waters would be cut off upon his arrival at the banks of the river. Joshua knew that if his guide said so it would be so.

He therefore marched the Israelites to the river. The waters "rose up in one heap a great way off" and "the people of Israel passed over on dry ground right against Jericho."

Nothing supernatural occurred. *But something psychic did occur.*

Joshua had then to capture the town of Jericho, and the spirit world gave him its aid.

"And it came to pass, when Joshua was near Jericho that he saw a man standing before him, holding a drawn sword."

Joshua went up to him and said, "Art thou for us, or art thou for our enemies?"

The man answered, "I am here as the captain of the host of Yahweh." Then, we are told, "Joshua fell on his face to the ground."

This "man" was either a fully materialized spirit, or was seen clairvoyantly and heard clairaudiently by Joshua. Yahweh had evidently sent him to assure Joshua that he had the support of the invisible, but invincible, host of heaven.

Yahweh then spoke to Joshua: "See, I have given into thine hand Jericho, and the king thereof, and the mighty men of valour," and gave him instructions for the capture of Jericho by psychic means.

For six successive days, the ark was to be carried in solemn procession round Jericho while seven priests blew their rams' horns.

On the seventh day, the circuit was to be made seven times, at the last of which the priests were to blow their trumpets, the people to shout and the walls of Jericho would fall down. And it was so.

It is a psychic story. I am not concerned with its historicity. But I am not prepared to pooh-pooh the psychic element in the story merely because anti-Spiritualist scholars do so. They tell us, of course, that the words "The wall fell down" are "literary hyperbole," merely meaning "victory."

I doubt it. But even if it were so, it would be ridiculous to suppose that the words "Joshua saw a man standing before him with his sword drawn" are "literary hyperbole."

We must remember that, according to the story, the "Captain of the host of Yahweh" had in hand the shattering of Jericho's wall. And we can well believe that there was some psychical reason for the seven days' circuit followed by the blast of trumpets and the shouting.

How can an anti-Spiritualist scholar understand a thoroughly Spiritualistic literature? St. Paul said, "The natural man receiveth not the things of the spirit; for they are foolishness to him, and he cannot know them, because they are spiritually discerned."

He might equally well have said, "The anti-Spiritualist cannot receive the things that are psychic; for they are foolishness to him, and he cannot know them, because they are psychically discerned."

Our next psychic story deals with Joshua's attack on the town of Ai. He was defeated with some loss. So he appealed to his guide, who told him that the defeat was due to an Israelite having transgressed the law.

A costly cloak, twenty-five pounds in silver and a bar of gold which were sacred property had been stolen, and Yahweh demanded their restoration.

Who was the thief? How was he discovered? He was discovered wholly by psychic means. Yahweh ordered Joshua to assemble the tribes of Israel before him at the sanctuary. We must bear in mind that each tribe had several clans. Each clan had several "houses." Each "house" had several individuals in it.

The thief was in one of the several houses of one of the several clans of one of the several tribes. No easy task to find him!

But Joshua assembled the tribes, entered the sanctuary, and, by the aid of the sacred oracular stones—Urim and Thummim—was able to separate the thief's tribe from the other tribes, his clan from the other clans, his house from the other houses, and finally the thief himself—Achan—from the other members of his house.

These psychic instruments—Urim and Thummim—gave accurate knowledge to an astonishing degree. Yet the scholars tell us that Joshua merely "cast lots." But if he merely "cast lots" then the whole story of his amazing discovery of the thief is sheer nonsense. It simply does not make sense.

But that is not all. The scholars actually refer us to the "Acts of the Apostles," where we are told that the disciples "cast lots" to decide who should fill Judas's place, "and the lot fell upon Matthias."

What a case to cite! It has absolutely nothing in common with those sacred oracular stones—Urim and Thummim—by means of which Yahweh gave instructions and made known his will.

The amusing part is that the scholars ridicule this "casting of lots" by the disciples, point out that they took good care to restrict the divine choice to two candidates and that the one on whom the lot fell was never heard of again!

But no sane person can ridicule Joshua's action in consulting Urim and Thummim, for they "delivered the goods"; they not only separated the thief from among thousands and thousands of Israelites, but led to the discovery, and restoration, of the stolen property.

Had it not been for Joshua's psychic powers of clairvoyance and clairaudience, and for his psychic instruments—Urim and Thummim—there would have been no story of Joshua to tell.

CHAPTER XXI

I WONDER how many persons in this country have heard of Deborah! She was every bit as great as Joan of Arc.

She was a military chieftain, a teacher, a judge, a patriot—and she "heard voices." By means of her psychic gifts, she was able to deliver Israel from the tyranny of King Jabin and all the host of Sisera.

As judge of Israel, she would sit under the famous

"Deborah palm-tree" in the highlands of Ephraim, deciding the cases brought to her by the Israelites. And, when King Jabin had for twenty years "mightily oppressed the children of Israel," it was to Deborah they came seeking deliverance.

So she "inquired of the Lord," who told her to send for one Barak and to tell him to go to Mount Tabor with ten thousand men, and the Lord would deliver the host of Sisera into his hands.

She at once summoned Barak to her presence, and evidently no one in Israel thought of disputing her authority, for he immediately came. She gave him his orders. But he feared to carry them out unless she would go with him. He was the type of man who finds it easier to believe in a woman than in the Lord.

He asked her to support him, and in her reply there is a touch of womanly scorn. She said to him, "I will certainly go with you but as you, a man, will not face the foe unsupported by a woman, the honour of victory shall not come to you; it shall be a woman's victory, the Lord shall sell Sisera into the hands of a woman."

How did she know that? She must have either seen it clairvoyantly, or heard it clairaudiently.

The prediction came true, and through the almost unexampled heroism of an unarmed woman the head of Sisera was broken and the power of King Jabin destroyed.

Had it not been for Deborah's psychic powers, we should never have heard of her, and might have heard no more of Israel. But her "voices" saved Israel, just as Joan's "voices" saved France.

Judge Deborah was succeeded by Judge Gideon.

While a judge lived, the people served Yahweh, but when the judge "died" they worshipped foreign gods, and the same story of oppression, deliverance, piety and idolatry was enacted again.

This time their idolatry led to the Lord delivering them into the hand of Midian for seven years. Who was to rescue them? A person who had the one essential qualification of being sufficiently psychic to "hear" the Lord. Without that qualification, little or nothing could be done.

In Gideon, the Lord found one who was a clairvoyant, clairaudient and materializing medium. And, when Gideon was "beating out wheat inside a winepress to hide it from the Midianites," a spirit guide suddenly appeared to him and said:

"The Lord is with thee, thou mighty man of valour . . . Go and save Israel from the hand of Midian."

This spirit guide was so human in appearance that Gideon could not make up his mind whether he was a materialized spirit or not. That will not surprise Spiritualists!

Well, Gideon asked for proof, and the spirit guide promptly produced fire from a rock. That, again, will not surprise Spiritualists. They have seen what spirit guides can do!

That same night, Gideon's faith was put to the test. The guide told him to deliver a blow to Israel's idolatry by "throwing down the altar of Baal that thy father hath." Gideon did so, and to his astonishment his father did not rebuke him.

And, when Gideon was preparing to resist an attack by Midian, we are told that "the spirit of the Lord came upon him. The Hebrew here reads, "A spirit from the Lord put on Gideon as a garment" i.e. "wore" him or "controlled" him.

The attack was imminent. There was no time to lose.

So the spirit guide controlled Gideon and gave orders that messengers were to be sent at once to rally the tribes of Israel, who responded to the call and assembled for battle.

But when Gideon, no longer under the control of the spirit, saw all this preparedness for war, his old doubts returned and he desired fresh proofs of the spirit's power.

He would lay a fleece of wool on the ground at night and if, in the morning, there was dew on the fleece and none on the ground, he would know that God meant to save Israel by his hand. And it was so.

But Gideon's sceptical mind was not quite satisfied, and he very politely asked the spirit guide if he would be so kind as to submit to one last test. This time he asked that the fleece might remain dry when the ground was wet with dew. And so it was.

How like ourselves were "them of old time"! They demanded proof. So do we. And the guides are as patient with us as with Gideon. But if we "test" them we must not be impatient when they test us.

Well, Gideon had now to submit to further tests of his faith. An army of 30,000 men had rallied round him when, suddenly, his spirit guide told him to reduce his numbers. The guide wanted the coming victory to be a God-given victory.

So he ordered Gideon to dismiss all who were "fearful and trembling." This reduced his army by 22,000. Still there were too many for the spirit's purpose, and Gideon was told to take the remaining 10,000 to the stream to drink.

No sooner had they reached the water's edge than 9,700 of them threw themselves on their faces and drank from the stream—thus exposing themselves to a possible sudden charge of Midianites. Only 300 drank cautiously, stooping quickly to dip their hands in the water and rising alert in their places again.

And the spirit said: "By the 300 men that lapped water from their hands will I save you." What a test! Gideon had to send the 9,700 back home.

However, that same night, the spirit guide told Gideon to steal down to the camp of Midian and listen to their talk.

This he did and overheard a Midianite "telling a dream unto his friend"—a flat round cake of barley-bread fell into the Midianite camp, and rolling on its edge like a wheel struck a tent and overturned it.

His friend interpreted this to mean that Midian would be destroyed by "a man of Israel."

Gideon realized, as he heard this, that there was fear within the camp of Midian. He at once returned to his own camp, divided his 300 men into three companies, gave each man a trumpet and a torch covered by a small jar, and stealthily surrounded the sleeping army of Midian.

Then, at a given sign, the torches flared up and the trumpets rang out while 300 voices shouted, "For God and for Gideon!"

Not a blow was struck. They stood still. And in frenzied panic the Midianites fled, believing themselves to be pursued, and that their fellow-fugitives were Israelites, and they turned their weapons against one another.

It was a God-given victory gained through the help of a great clairvoyant, clairaudient, and materializing medium—Gideon the Judge.

And now we come to Judge Jephthah. Heaven only knows why he was "chosen" to lead Israel, but heaven *does* know. He was chosen because he possessed the psychic faculty—"the Spirit of the Lord came upon him."

He was no saint. He had been the leader of a band of robbers. He was the son of a harlot and for that cause had been driven out of his home.

But, would God choose a robber even if he did possess psychic gifts? Well, even a robber may have much hidden good in him. Jephthah had had a hard life. His brothers' attitude may have embittered him, and inclined him to lead the life of a freebooter. God makes allowances for men's disadvantages.

And Jephthah's people were prepared to do so too when they found that Gilead was threatened with an attack by Ammonites. His own tribe, which had driven him out, came pleading with him to return and defend their territory. He agreed, and a spirit guide supported him as he marched out to attack the Ammonites.

But on his way, he made a very foolish vow that, if Yahweh would give him victory, he would offer up as a thanksgiving to him whoever came out of his house to welcome him on his return.

Poor man, he had no idea that such human sacrifices were abhorrent to Yahweh. He had seen, when in exile, that men offered up their children to Moloch when they wanted victory.

Well, he defeated the Ammonites, and, on his return, his daughter, an only child, ran out to meet him. He was horrified, and exclaimed, "I have vowed to the Lord, and I cannot go back."

But his heroic daughter comforted him by saying, "Father, if you have vowed unto the Lord, you must keep the vow."

Had it not been for Jephthah's psychic gift, we should

never have heard of him or his daughter, and the whole course of Israel's history might have been changed by the Ammonites defeating the Children of Israel.

CHAPTER XXII

OUR next psychic story contains an account of a remarkable materialization.

A spirit guide materialized and spoke to Manoah's wife, telling her that she would bear a son (Samson), and to be careful not to drink wine or eat unclean food because the child was to be consecrated to God from birth, and would begin the deliverance of Israel from the Philistines.

So remarkable was this materialization that the woman seems to have thought that the spirit was a living man who claimed superior knowledge of God's workings.

She told her husband about it, and he was naturally anxious to meet the man who had said such strange things to his wife.

The spirit guide came again to the woman "as she sat in the field," and she ran to fetch her husband who "came up to the man" and said to him, "Art thou the man who spakest to my wife?" And he said, "I am." Manoah "knew not that he was an angel of the Lord."

Manoah then invited him to stay and dine with them. But he replied, "If you are going to dine, offer the food as a burnt offering unto the Lord rather than give it to me."

So Manoah "took a kid with the meat-offering and offered it up upon the rock unto the Lord . . . and, when the flame rose to heaven . . . the angel ascended in the flame."

This means that the spirit guide dematerialized behind the screen of smoke. Manoah and his wife then knew that he had been a fully materialized spirit.

And that is the psychic preface to the story of Samson.

The child Samson was from birth consecrated to the service of Jehovah, and when he grew up "the spirit of the Lord began to move him," i.e., he gradually became conscious of his psychic gift.

He judged Israel for twenty years and is reported to have done many wonderful deeds. But he misused his gift. However, he attributed the success of his exploits to spirit power, and the narrator did so too.

For many years after the "death" of Samson, there was a dearth of clairaudient and clairvoyant mediums. "The word of the Lord was precious in those days; there was no open vision."

The Hebrew here is, "A word from the Lord was *rare* in those days; there was no *frequent* vision." This means that there were few clairaudients who could hear a word from the Lord, and few clairvoyants.

This fallow period ended in the birth of one of the greatest mediums—Samuel. His mother, Hannah, had dedicated him from his birth to the service of the Temple, and he attended upon Eli, the high priest, whom he eventually succeeded in office.

His first psychic experience came to him when a boy. He was asleep in the Temple near the ark of God, that battery of psychic power, when he heard a voice clairaudiently, but thought it was Eli calling him. But Eli said he had not called him.

Three times did the voice call him by name. Both he and Eli were greatly puzzled by it, for Eli was not clairaudient and "Samuel did not yet know the Lord, neither was the word of the Lord yet revealed to him." Samuel had not yet *seen* his spirit guide, nor *heard* him speak.

Eli began to suspect that the voice might be "a word from the Lord," which had become so rare in his day. So he bade Samuel go back to bed, and, if he heard the voice again, to say "Speak, Lord, for thy servant heareth."

This time "The Lord *came* and *stood*, and *called*, Samuel," and from that moment Samuel "knew the Lord" and "the word of the Lord was revealed to him."

The message given by this spirit guide to the little boy did not apply to him, but to Eli. It was a terrifying message. He was to tell Eli that his sons were blaspheming God, that though Eli knew they were doing so he had done nothing to check them, and that, therefore, his household would be punished for ever.

Why did not the spirit guide tell Eli? Why frighten a boy with such a message? *Because the boy could "hear"; the boy was a medium. The old priest was not a medium.*

Poor little Samuel was afraid to give Eli the guide's message. But Eli said to him, "What was it that the Lord told you? God kill you and worse if you hide from me a single word of what he told you!" So Samuel told him everything.

"It is the Lord," said Eli, "let him do what seemeth him good." And "the Lord was with Samuel and let none of his words become ineffectual or unfulfilled."

And when he became a man "All Israel knew that Samuel was established to be a prophet of the Lord," i.e., a divinely accredited medium and leader of Israel.

Whenever a prophet arises, the priest takes a subordinate place. For, unless a priest be also a prophet, he cannot "know the Lord" or have "the word of the Lord revealed to him."

It matters not how righteous a priest may be, he cannot, unless he is a medium, contact the world of spirit and get to know God's will for His age and generation.

At Shiloh, Samuel again saw a spirit guide, whom he knew to be the one that had spoken to him in the Temple because he told him so—"The Lord *appeared* and *revealed* himself to Samuel by the *word* of the Lord." It is obvious that Samuel was clairvoyant as well as clairaudient.

The prophecy that Eli's household should be punished for ever was fulfilled when the Philistines defeated Israel, killed Eli's two sons, and captured the Ark.

The fame of the Ark extended beyond Israel, for the Philistines were afraid when they heard that Israel had brought it into the camp, and they cried, "God is come into the camp of Israel." And, after they had captured it, evil befell them wherever they took it, till, at length, out of sheer terror, they returned it to Israel.

Israel now asked for a king. "We will have a King over us; that he may rule over us, march in front of us, and fight our battles." They wanted a leader who was a fighter, and told Samuel so.

He at once spoke to his spirit guide, who was grieved to hear it. But, knowing that the people were determined to have their own way, he instructed Samuel to grant their request, but, at the same time, to warn them of all that it would mean to have an earthly king to rule over them.

So Samuel had now to find the man best fitted to be king. His guide knew that mere brute strength, or military prowess, was no qualification for kingship.

And, as we shall see, the man chosen by Samuel to be king was a man who possessed the psychic faculty.

A man had lost his asses and asked his son to go, with a servant, to look for them, but they could not be found. The servant then suggested a visit to a well-known seer, who might be able to "see" where the asses had strayed.

But the son, whose name was Saul, said, "We have no money for the fee!"

"Yes," said the servant, "I have ninepence."

"Good," said Saul. "Come and let us go."

On entering the city, they met Samuel, whose guide had told him *the day before*, that on the morrow he would meet a young man whom he was to anoint king. As soon as Samuel saw Saul, his guide said, "Here is the man."

The whole of what follows is extraordinarily interesting to Spiritualists.

Samuel invited Saul and his servant to dine with him and to stay the night, promising that in the morning he would tell Saul "all that was in his mind." In other words, Samuel would give Saul a "sitting," for he knew that Saul was far more worried about the tyranny of the Philistines than about the lost donkeys.

However, he told Saul not to worry about the asses as they were already found. How did Samuel know this? He must either have seen it clairvoyantly, or heard it clairaudiently from his guide.

In the dining-hall, Samuel seated Saul at the head of thirty guests, and treated him "right royally." In the morning he accompanied Saul to the outskirts of the town, and said to him, "Tell the servant to go on ahead; but stop here yourself that I may unfold to you God's message."

Then Samuel, taking a flask of oil, poured it over his

head and kissed him, saying, "Hath not the Lord anointed you to be King over his people of Israel?" And, in anticipation of Saul's doubts, Samuel assured him that certain "signs" would be given which would convince him that the Lord had anointed him.

How the anti-Spiritualists would laugh at these "signs" and sneer at their "triviality"! But to Saul they were irrefutable proof.

The "signs" predicted by Samuel were these:

Saul would meet two men, who would tell him that the asses had been found.

He would then meet three men, one carrying three kids, one carrying three loaves of bread, one carrying a bottle of wine. They would salute him and give him two loaves.

After that, he would meet a band of prophets, and would himself prophesy and be "turned into another man."

And "all those signs came to pass that day."

CHAPTER XXIII

SAUL was "turned into another man" when he found himself possessed of the psychic faculty and able to prophesy; it was the turning-point in his life.

"*And when the people who knew Saul of old saw that he prophesied, they said one to another, What is this that is come unto the son of Kish? Is Saul also among the prophets?*"

The people were clamouring for a king, and Samuel told them quite plainly that in demanding an earthly king they were rejecting Yahweh's guidance. But they would not listen to reason.

He summoned them, and Saul was chosen king. Saul, however, could not be found; he was hiding. So the people *decided to ask their spirit guide*, through a medium, where Saul was. And they were told, "Behold he hath hid himself among the stuff," and they ran and fetched him.

Saul was found solely by psychic means, and he was "chosen" solely because he possessed the psychic faculty.

But he was untrue to his trust. He disobeyed the command of the spirit who had told him to remain at Gilgal and not to prepare an attack on the Philistines until he had received further instructions through Samuel.

But Saul grew impatient and prepared for battle. When Samuel came, he said to him, "Saul, thou hast done a senseless thing; if thou hadst obeyed the command of Yahweh, he would have established thy kingdom for ever. But now thy kingdom shall not stand. Yahweh has already found a man who will obey him, and he has appointed him king over Israel."

There is no graver sin than for a prophet, priest or king to disobey the divine commands. However psychically gifted a man may be, God cannot compel that man to obey Him.

He can only test him. Saul did not stand up to the test and was therefore rejected. "*Because thou hast rejected the word of the Lord, he hath rejected thee from being king.*"

Saul's natural successor was his eldest son Jonathan—a strong and beautiful character, popular and patriotic. Why did not the spirit choose him to succeed Saul? Because he lacked the one essential quality—the psychic faculty.

The Bible makes it clear that Mankind's greatest need is for revelation from the spirit world, and revelation can be received only through the exercise of the psychic faculty.

Comparatively few persons possess this faculty, but those few are of supreme value to God, for they are the only instruments through which His will can be made known to Mankind.

"Would God that *all* the Lord's people were prophets," said Moses.

See now how Samuel's gift of clairaudience enabled him to discover the man *whom his spirit guide had appointed* to be the new king over Israel.

Samuel heard his guide say to him, "Go to Jesse . . . I have provided me a king from among his sons. . . Anoint the one whom I point out to you."

He obeyed and went. Jesse had seven sons, and Samuel felt sure that the tall, good-looking son—Eliab—was the one selected by the Lord. But his guide said, "The Lord hath not chosen any of these."

Samuel was puzzled indeed, and asked Jesse whether he had any other sons.

"Yes, the youngest, who is a shepherd—he is with the flock," said Jesse, who was told to send for him. The moment Samuel saw the boy, his spirit guide said to him, "Arise. Anoint him, for this is he. And the spirit of the Lord came mightily upon David from that day forward." The Hebrew says, "*a* spirit *from* the Lord came . . ."

David was "chosen" because he was a medium.

When Goliath issued his challenge, David said, "Who is this that dares to defy the armies of the *living* God?"

God was to him a living person, his spirit guide,

whom he had seen and heard. He could therefore triumphantly cry out to Goliath, "I come to thee in the name of the living guide of Israel's armies, and I will smite thee."

What gave David this certainty of victory? He had, of course, either seen clairvoyantly, or heard clairaudiently, that he would slay the giant. And it was so.

Again, when the women sang, "Saul hath slain his thousands, and David his ten thousands," which roused Saul's jealousy, causing David to flee for his life, David "inquired of the Lord" or "sat to the Lord" at every turn throughout his life in exile.

When the Philistines were attacking Keilah he asked his guide, "Shall I go and smite them?"

His guide said, "Yes." But David's men were afraid, for his guide had not said definitely that David would win. So David "inquired" again, and this time his guide told him, "I will deliver the Philistines into thine hand."

The men were satisfied and a great victory was won. David occupied Keilah, and Saul heard of it and sent an army to besiege the city. The news reached David. He consulted his guide and was told to vacate the city immediately. This he did.

"*And Saul sought his life every day.*" And every day David's spirit guide saved him from the hand of Saul.

Again, when the Amalekites had burned the city of Ziklag and taken captive all the women—including David's two wives—and when in anger "the people spake of stoning David," he "strengthened himself in the Lord his God."

How? He held a séance or, as the Bible puts it, "inquired of the Lord." He asked his guide three questions, "Shall I pursue the Amalekites? Shall I be able to overtake them? Shall I recover all they have taken?"

"Yes," said his guide, and we read "David smote them and rescued all the women, and his two wives, and brought back all."

Spiritualists will understand this. But the scholars, alas, knowing nothing of the psychic side of life, cannot understand it. So they are obliged to reduce objective clairaudience to the subjective auditory something which they call "the inward ear"; and, likewise to reduce objective clairvoyance to the subjective, discerning something which they call "the eye of the soul."

In saying this I do not in any way under-estimate the value of the poetry of the spiritual life. But psychical phenomena are not poetry, they are FACTS.

No character in the Old Testament kept in closer contact with his spirit guide than did David. He "sat before the Lord" whenever an important step had to be taken, or decision arrived at.

I use the phrase "sat before the Lord" because it is used in 2 Sam. vii. 18, and curiously enough nowhere else. The scholars think it means a special "attitude of devotion." I doubt it.

Far more likely is it to mean what a Spiritualist means when he says, "I had a sitting," or "I sat," especially when we are told that David "went in and sat"; he "went in" to the tent, the sacred séance room, in which the Ark was housed in the citadel of David.

After the "death" of King Saul, David "inquired of the Lord" and was told to go at once to the chief city of Judah. He obeyed. And the men of Judah anointed him King.

Later he was anointed King of all Israel, and the Philistines made an overwhelming attack on him.

He retreated and "inquired of the Lord" who said, "Attack them. I will deliver them into thy hands." He obeyed and won a great victory.

The Philistines rallied and again attacked. David again "inquired of the Lord" who now said, "Attack them not; make a circuit behind them, and it shall be when thou hearest a movement in the top of the balsam trees, that then thou shalt bestir thyself, for then is the Lord gone out before thee to smite the hosts of the Philistines."

The tree-tops would give the signal for the advance! Why not?

I was seated in the shade of a tree one summer's afternoon when there seemed to be not a breath of air anywhere. My companion, who was a medium and also the brother of a distinguished Church dignitary, said to me, "Have you ever conversed with a guide through the medium of a leaf?"

"Never," said I.

A branch covered with leaves was hanging just above our heads, and my companion pointing to one of the larger leaves said, "We will 'get in touch' through that one."

He then asked his guide if he was present, and the leaf moved up and down three times, signifying "Yes" —just as does the table.

It spelt out sentence after sentence and we had quite a long conversation with my companion's guide through that leaf, while the other leaves remained motionless.

If such things can happen in our day, why not in David's day? Was Yahweh less powerful than my companion's guide?

Sceptics may scorn, scholars may scoff, but what really matters is this: Through "a movement of a leaf" we received much valuable assistance from a spirit guide, and through "a movement in the tops of the trees" David received much valuable information from his spirit guide.

CHAPTER XXIV

THE Bible tells of a certain good and pure woman whose psychic gifts were so remarkable that the whole countryside rang with the fame of them.

The Church calls her a "witch." The Bible never calls her a witch; it calls her a *woman*. And, curiously enough the Greek equivalent of the Hebrew word for "woman" is the very word used by Jesus when addressing his mother! The deduction is obvious!

The Woman of Endor was no witch; she was a beautiful character, as I shall show. But the Church would have us conjure up the witch's cavern—dark and eerie, the horrible old witch with dishevelled hair and ragged dirty skirt, the blue fire and the cauldrons, the secret spells and incantations.

I say the "Church" because it is the Church that interprets the Bible to us, that calls this gifted, honourable, courageous, generous-hearted and compassionate woman a "witch."

On the other hand, no self-respecting, trustworthy, honest and unprejudiced reader of the Bible, however much he might deprecate Spiritualist practices, could possibly regard this woman as anything but a good and highly gifted person. Here is the story:

Samuel had "died." King Saul had suppressed the mediums. The Philistine hosts had struck terror in

Saul's heart—"his heart trembled greatly." He "inquired of the Lord," but the Lord answered him not.

So under cover, disguised, he consulted the famous, though suppressed, medium at Endor, and asked her to try and get into touch with "whomsoever I shall name unto thee."

She politely refused. To her it seemed a snare, a ruse to entrap her. So Saul assured her that "no punishment shall happen to thee."

His haggard and distressed countenance evidently inclined her to employ her great gift, though she obviously knew that the word of a chance stranger was unsafe ground to go upon.

She asked no fee but simply said, "Whom shall I try and contact?"

"I need Samuel," said Saul.

And "when the woman saw Samuel," who revealed to her who the chance stranger was, she exclaimed, "Thou art Saul. Why hast thou deceived me?"

We may here note that the statement in I Chron. x. 13, is the *priestly* chronicler's homily upon the story in I Sam. xxviii, and is quite inaccurate. It reads, "And Saul died . . . because he asked counsel of one that had a familiar spirit . . . and inquired not of the Lord."

Nothing of the kind! Saul did "*inquire of the Lord*" *and he* "*died,*" *not because he consulted a medium, but because the Philistines slew him.*

The King said, "Be not afraid; what do you see?"

She answered, "I see a spirit building up, he is an old man wearing a mantle." The "mantle" gave the clue, for had not Saul "torn it" at his last meeting with the prophet? And Saul knew it was Samuel, and bowed with his face to the ground.

Samuel then spoke to Saul—either through the medium, or in the direct voice, or he was heard by her clairaudiently—and asked why he had sought him. And Saul told him that the Philistines were upon him, that he was "sore distressed," and that his spirit-guide had departed from him.

And Samuel said, "What is the good of your coming to me when you know that your guide has departed from you because, as I so often told you, you disobeyed him, you 'rejected the word of the Lord, and he hath also rejected thee from being King,' and 'to-morrow shalt thou and thy sons with thee be slain by the Philistines.' "

And it was so.

Had the woman been fraudulent she would never have given Saul such a terrifying message as that he would be defeated in battle and slain with his two sons on the morrow. She would have spoken none but fair words to the King, knowing that her life was in his hands. But she was a thoroughly genuine and courageous medium.

Saul was so staggered by the message that he fell prostrate to the ground. And the woman's one thought was to restore him. She was eager to prepare him a meal. But what delicate courtesy there was in the manner of her proposal!

She made it a favour to herself. She begged him to accept the meal, as some return for her sacrifice in risking her life by holding the séance.

Remember, she had asked no fee, and the only reward she asked in payment for her sacrifice was that she might be given the opportunity of feeding a faint and exhausted man who had taken away her livelihood.

None but a most beautiful character could have uttered the words, "Behold, thine handmaid hath hearkened unto thy voice; and I have put my life in my hand, and have hearkened unto thy words which thou spakest unto me.

"Now, therefore, I pray thee, hearken thou also unto the voice of thine handmaid, and let me set a meal before thee; and eat, that thou mayest have strength, when thou goest on thy way."

Her character was revealed once for all when she begged Saul, as if asking a personal boon, to allow her to prepare a meal.

A coarse nature would have shrunk coldly from a man who had destroyed her livelihood and had been rejected by God and was doomed to "die" on the morrow. But there was no touch of coarseness in the heart of this sweet woman, who saw in the anguish of even a guilty and God-forsaken man a reason for kind attentions and self-denying service.

The woman who anointed the feet of Jesus won the compensation that her name should be remembered wherever the Gospel should be preached. And this banned Woman of Endor has won the compensation that the Bible has so faithfully recorded her character that, whenever a self-respecting reader honestly studies it, his heart goes out to her with a tribute of admiration and gratitude.

But the Church, in her ignorance, calls this good woman a "witch" and in her latest commentary, "A New Commentary on Holy Scripture," suggests that her prejudice has altogether warped her judgment.

Sixty-one of her best scholars have contributed to this commentary and, when they are dealing with subjects of which they have expert knowledge, their judgment is usually sound.

Let me quote what this book has to say about the story of the Woman of Endor and submit the quotation to the fair-minded judgment of self-respecting Englishmen:

> "The story attests the widespread belief in necromancy in Israel. . . . It was believed that the spirits of of the dead still retained the outward semblance of their former selves, were acquainted with what took place on earth, and exercised a powerful influence on the fortunes of their descendants. . . It was only as a last desperate expedient, that King Saul had recourse to this 'black magic.' . . . The medium pretended to see a ghost which she described, but her dupes only heard a voice, which by ventriloquism seemed to come from the ground."

And that is Church scholarship!!

But is it honest? Is it sincere? If it is, I fail to see the use of Church theological colleges, theological professors, and professors of Biblical exegesis. If the Church colleges can so stultify the mind, blind the reason, and destroy sound judgment as to produce this kind of scholarship, the sooner we close such colleges the better.

For consider: Intelligent, reasonable, cultured and sincere men, including such famous men as F. W. H. Myers, Alfred Russel Wallace, William Crookes, William Barrett, W. J. Crawford, William James, James Hyslop, Lombroso, Notzing, de Morgan, Flammarion, Gustave Geley, Marshall Hall, Conan Doyle, Oliver Lodge, and many others, all testify to the fact that

(*a*) The spirits of the "dead" still retain the outward semblance of their former selves.

(*b*) Are acquainted with what took place on earth.

(*c*) Exercise a powerful influence on the fortunes of their descendants.

Consider further: We are asked to believe by the ecclesiastical editors of the *New Commentary*, that these intelligent, reasonable, cultured and sincere men, including the famous men whose names I have quoted, scientists, psychologists, king's counsellors, astronomers, doctors, criminologists, have had recourse to "black magic," and that all—hundreds of them!—were duped by mediums who pretended to see ghosts which they described, but their "dupes only heard voices, which by ventriloquism seemed to come from the ground."

Self-respecting, intelligent, fair-minded and sincere-minded persons will not feel inclined to accept so inane a judgment, though they may quite easily come to regard our theological seminaries as "mental prisons" rather than colleges.

CHAPTER XXV

DAVID sinned. He stole another man's wife. And, in order to get rid of Uriah, her husband, David gave orders to his commander-in-chief, Joab, to "set Uriah in the forefront of the hottest battle . . . that he may be smitten, and die." And it was so.

How comes it then that we read, "David did that which was right in the eyes of the Lord, and turned not aside from anything that He had commanded all the days of his life," and that "the heart of David was perfect with the Lord," for he was "a man after God's own heart"?

Wherein did David do that which was right? In what sense was his heart perfect? He did that which was right in that he never ceased to "inquire of the

Lord," to hold sacred séances. And his heart was perfect in his trustful and obedient attitude towards his guide, Yahweh, and his commands.

If on one occasion David sinned against two human spirits he did not commit the sin against the Holy Spirit; he did not cut himself off from communication with the spirit-world or deny its inspiration.

Perfection is an attitude, an aim. The absolute perfection of God is not attainable, but absolute trust which is perfect—relatively to a man's capacity and condition—is. And David's trust in Yahweh was perfect in that sense. That is why Yahweh "loved" him.

Yahweh "loved" also David's son—Solomon. What does this word "loved" mean? We are told that when Solomon was born "the Lord loved him." This was not the general love which he would have for all infants. It was rather a rejoicing over one whom he knew to be psychically gifted from birth.

Yahweh always "loved" those whom he knew he could *use*, those to whom he could speak, those who had the "open vision," those through whom he could make known his will, those who would communicate with him and obey him.

"And Solomon loved the Lord, walking in the statutes of David his father" and exercising his psychic faculty as did David. He was not the eldest son. He was the mediumistic son. For that reason was he "chosen."

Solomon celebrated his accession to the throne by a great religious ceremony at the Gibeon psychic centre, and, at night, Yahweh "appeared to him in a dream" and had an extremely important conversation with him.

An orthodox commentator tells us that in this dream "Solomon was vouchsafed a theophany." Such language is unintelligible. The scholar uses it because the words "Yahweh appeared in a dream" are double-Dutch to him. He knows nothing of such appearances. So he uses the good old Greek word "theophany" to express what is "Greek" to him. It would be highly amusing were it not so pathetic.

This appearance of Yahweh was an objective appearance. The dream was more than a dream, for we are told that "the Lord appeared to Solomon the second time, as he had appeared unto him at Gibeon," and, on this second occasion Yahweh had another extremely important conversation with Solomon. Obviously then it was not an ordinary dream!

The reason why, at a later date, "the Lord was angry with Solomon" was because he had disobeyed the commands of Yahweh "who had appeared unto him twice." Solomon was clairvoyant and clairaudient.

When the narrator tells us that "Divine wisdom was in Solomon," and "Yahweh gave Solomon wisdom," and "Yahweh put wisdom into his heart," he is merely recording the happy result of Solomon having exercised his psychic gifts.

David had given his son Solomon the pattern of the temple he wished him to build. Where did David get the pattern from? Let David tell us. He says: "Every detail of the pattern I have received *in writing* from the hand of the Lord."

These words utterly baffle the orthodox scholars who, in their bewilderment, translate them thus, "All these plans I have been inspired to write down by the Lord who instructed me."

Are we then to understand that those who are engaged in the sacred work of translating and interpreting the Bible for us have been "inspired and instructed by the Lord"? They would be the last persons to use such words in connexion with their work.

Yet they use them in reference to David's work. Why? Because the Hebrew compels them; they cannot reduce it to lower terms, though the terms convey nothing to them.

The scholars knowing little of automatic writing, and less of spirit writing, are nonplussed by the words "in writing from the hand of the Lord." They admit that "the hand of the Lord" is "a frequent expression for the prophetic trance," but they cannot connect "writing" with the "trance" condition.

So to suit their own convenience, and ignorance, they deliberately mistranslate David's words. David did not say, "All these plans I have been inspired to write down, etc." He said, "Every detail of the pattern I have received in writing from the hand of the Lord."

He meant that he had received the pattern through spirit writing just as we to-day receive messages and writings from the spirit world. In our psychic circles we provide our spirit friends with paper or slate and pencil. They do the writing.

Sometimes there is no need for a pencil; they can quite easily write without one. But no physical assistance whatever is given by the sitters; it is purely spirit writing.

"ELIJAH'S LETTER"—that is how the scholars describe the *spirit writing* received by King Jehoram from Elijah the prophet. The narrator says, "And there came a writing to King Jehoram from Elijah the prophet, saying, Thus saith the Lord . . ."

Elijah had been in the spirit world for some years, certainly not less than four years, and he now conveys through the medium of spirit writing, the Lord's condemnation of the King's actions. That is what the Bible says.

But to the mind of the orthodox biblical scholar it is unthinkable. Of course it is, for he has no "terms" in which to think such a thing.

So he affirms that Elijah must have been in the flesh when King Jehoram received the writing, and that the second book of Kings cannot be chronologically correct when it tells us that Elijah was "translated" into the spirit world at least four years before Jehoram came to the throne.

So we have "Elijah's Letter" instead of "ELIJAH'S SPIRIT WRITING." Once again: Only a Spiritualist can understand the Spiritualistic literature which we call the Bible.

Solomon tells us that "the Lord hath said that he would dwell in *thick darkness*." Now, what can that mean? It is, of course, another utterance bearing on the production of psychic phenomena.

It is well to remember that human beings are fashioned in darkness, and that darkness is essential to the early development of certain plants. And in the phases of psychic activity such as direct voice, ectoplasmic lights and materialization there is a *creative process* which darkness greatly assists.

That is why the "inner shrine" was in "thick darkness." And in that darkness the luminous cloud which "filled the temple, so that the priests could not stand to serve," was generated and the direct voice produced.

It is very instructive to note the occasion on which Solomon said, "The Lord hath said that he would dwell in thick darkness." It was immediately after the priests had come out of the "holy place" and found that the "cloud," the luminous ectoplasmic cloud, had filled the temple, "for the glory of the Lord filled the House of the Lord."

It was *then* that Solomon said, "The Lord hath said that he would dwell in thick darkness." It was as if he had said, "The Lord hath fulfilled his promise. We obeyed the words of the Lord and did darken the sacred room, and the Lord hath now given unto us the visible token of his abiding presence."

I wonder what would happen to-day were a priest to construct, without anyone knowing it, a completely darkened inner shrine within his church, with the result that a luminous cloud filled the church.

The people would be terrified just as they would be were they to witness a repetition of the Pentecostal wind, with the shaking, the tongues of fire, and the foreign tongues; or, any of the psychic phenomena mentioned in the Old Testament and New Testament.

There is an entire absence of any visible, supernormal sign of God's presence in the orthodox churches of today. They have no belief in the "signs and wonders" and the "greater works" promised by Jesus to his followers. They are as opposed to any outward, visible, supernormal manifestation of God's presence as they are to objective manifestations of the so-called dead.

They refuse to "disturb the dead." And they refuse to disturb their dead dogmas, doctrines, threats, forms, ceremonies and church services. If they would but "darken their lightness" it might "lighten their darkness."

CHAPTER XXVI

THE purpose of this book is to show that the Bible is full of psychic happenings which the narrators attribute to the psychic gifts of the mediums in conjunction with the supernormal power of the spirit world.

In this book I am not concerned with the historicity of the psychic stories, but only with the fact that they are narrated as *psychic* stories which, unless given a psychic interpretation, do not make sense.

At Solomon's "death," the kingdom of Israel split in two. His son, Rehoboam, ruled over Judah in the South. Jeroboam, the Ephraimite, ruled over Israel in the North.

Rehoboam was determined to defeat Jeroboam, and had gathered an army of 180,000 picked men to attack Israel. *A message from the spirit world prevented the attack.*

It was heard clairaudiently by one Shemaiah, who at once conveyed it to Rehoboam. The message ran, "Speak unto Rehoboam, the son of Solomon, King of Judah, and to all the people saying, Thus saith the Lord, Ye shall not go up, nor fight against thy brethren the children of Israel: return every man to his house." And they did so.

This does not imply that the people were superstitious. It merely shows with what reverence they regarded the "word of the Lord" heard *clairaudiently* by Shemaiah the prophet. The people were familiar with the psychic faculty and believed in guidance from the spirit world.

The belief dominated their thought and action, and was by far the most potent factor in their life. And this prophet Shemaiah would never have been heard of had he not been a medium through whom the Lord spake; indeed, we never hear of him again.

We now meet another medium. He is referred to as "a man of God," and we should never have heard of him had he not foretold the coming of Josiah 350 years before he came.

Such a prophecy so bewilders the minds of commentators that they endeavour to get rid of it by deleting the name Josiah, or resolving it into something more general.

Knowing little or nothing of the marvels of clairvoyance, and other psychic gifts, our commentators are ever ready to delete, or "spiritualize" out of existence, those parts of the Bible which cannot be made to fit in with their preconceived ideas and narrow outlook.

This is the story of the "man of God." King Jeroboam was offering illegal sacrifice before the altar at Bethel. The "man of God" came to him and denounced this idolatrous worship, saying that he had heard *clairaudiently*, "by the word of the Lord" that a child would be born to the house of David, "Josiah by name," who would sacrifice upon that very altar the priests who dared to burn incense upon it (the prophecy was fulfilled in the reign of King Josiah).

Jeroboam was furious when he heard it, and "he raised his hand from the altar" and said, "Arrest him." But something had happened to his hand, for "he could not draw it back again to him." Also, "the altar split and the ashes poured out from the altar."

Jeroboam was terror-stricken and besought the "man of God" to entreat the Lord "that my hand may be restored me again." He did so, and the hand was restored.

In gratitude and awe the king invited the prophet to dine with him and accept a fee. But the prophet refused saying, "The Lord hath charged me that I eat no bread, nor drink water, neither return by the way that I came." So he departed by another way.

News of the fidelity of the man of God to his commission reached the ears of "an old prophet in Bethel" who sought him and, finding him sitting under an oak, said to him, "Come home with me and eat bread." But the man of God again refused as the Lord had commanded him.

The old prophet then said, "An angel spake unto me saying, Bring him back with thee into thine house, that he may eat bread and drink water." It was a lie. But, unfortunately, the man of God believed the lie and went home with the old prophet.

And as they sat at table a genuine "word of the Lord" came to the old man who had lied, saying, "Tell the man of God, Thus saith the Lord, Forasmuch as thou hast been disobedient and hast not obeyed the Lord, but camest back, and hast eaten bread and drunk water, thou shalt not be buried in the sepulchre of thy fathers."

And after he had eaten and drunk, the man of God went out, but a lion met him on the way and killed him.

The story shows that, in those days, no sin was deemed greater than that of disobedience to a personal, direct command from the spirit-world. The man of God had trusted the second-hand revelation of another man (and it happened to be a lie) rather than that which had been given directly to himself.

Now we come to a blind man, who was a "seer." King Jeroboam's son fell ill, and he sent his wife, disguised as a common woman, to consult the blind prophet Abijah who "shall tell thee how the child is to fare."

Meanwhile, the prophet's guide had told him that, "The wife of Jeroboam cometh to inquire of thee concerning her son; for he is sick: thus and thus shalt thou say unto her."

So when she knocked at the door the prophet said, "Come in, thou art Jeroboam's wife, why hast thou disguised thyself?" He then told her that his guide had charged him to convey grave news to her which she would find hard to bear.

Her son would "die" before she reached home, and the house of Jeroboam would be utterly swept away "as a man sweepeth away refuse, till all is gone." Who but a medium in close touch with the spirit world would have known these things, and have had the courage to declare them?

It has been said that Jesus Himself was a far greater miracle than all His miracles put together. The same may be said of Elijah.

And just because he was an outstanding person, we are not surprised to find that he possessed outstanding psychic powers—powers which are incredible to those who have little knowledge of the psychic faculty, and truly amazing, but by no means incredible, to those who have.

He first declared his power by telling King Ahab that, "There shall be neither dew nor rain except as I give orders." Why did he tell him that?

Because Ahab was ruining the religion of Israel by allowing the idolatrous worship of the idol Melkart, and had incurred Yahweh's threatened punishment for idolatry to "shut up the skies so that no rain shall fall, and your land shall yield no produce, and ye shall quickly die."

And no rain fell until the third year of the famine.

The Lord, the spirit guide of Elijah, made provision for him by telling him to hide himself by the brook Cherith, "and it shall be that thou shalt drink of the brook; and I have commanded the ravens to feed thee there. . . . And the ravens brought him bread and flesh in the morning, and bread and flesh in the evening; and he drank of the brook."

Some commentators have attempted to minimise this super-normal occurrence by substituting the words "the Arabs" for "the ravens," but the Hebrew word means "ravens" and nothing else.

Spiritualists who are familiar with the "signs and wonders" of the séance room, e.g., the transportation of material objects without material agency, commonly called apports, will not deem it impossible for ravens to feed a man.

Spiritualists know that the power of the spirit world is beyond imagination, and every day new powers are being revealed to them. They humbly live and learn as students of the science of the supernormal.

The brook soon dried up; there was no rain. So the spirit guide told Elijah to go to Zarephath where "I have commanded a widow to sustain thee." When he reached the gate of the town, there was the widow gathering some sticks!

He called out to her, "Pray fetch me a little water and a bite of food." But she told him that she had nothing but a handful of meal in a jar and a little oil in a flask.

"Fear not," said Elijah, "go and cook the meal for yourselves; but first make a little cake of it here for me. The Lord has promised that your jar of meal shall not be used up, nor shall the flask of oil give out, before He sends rain on the land."

And the widow, her boy, and Elijah were thus sustained by "the meal that wasted not, and the flask of oil that failed not."

Hitherto, the mother and her boy had starved, and we are not surprised to read that the boy was near unto "death." But Elijah prayed and gave the boy treatment, and he recovered.

Jesus fed the multitude by causing the bread to fail not. Elijah fed his friends by causing the meal to fail not. Jesus healed the sick. Elijah healed the sick. If the so-called miracles of Jesus prove His deity, the so-called miracles of Elijah prove *his* deity.

CHAPTER XXVII

ELIJAH was a dematerializing medium. That is why he is regarded as the most weird and mysterious figure among the prophets.

He appears on the scene unheralded. No hint is given as to his birth or parentage. He is a rugged Bedouin who has a habit of suddenly appearing and disappearing.

Elijah was one of the most courageous mediums who ever lived. He was Yahweh's relentless champion. Israel had been seduced into worshipping a foreign god named Melkart. And Elijah was raised up to save the situation.

With eagle-like suddenness, Elijah appeared before Ahab, King of Israel, and announced that the hearts of this apostate king and people were to be chastened by a drought which would last as long as he deemed necessary. The drought came.

Jezebel, the king's wife, who had established the worship of the idol Melkart in Israel, promptly "slew the prophets of the Lord." Elijah escaped, and Ahab hunted him to slay him.

In the third year of the drought, Elijah received clairaudiently a message from Yahweh telling him to go to King Ahab. Meanwhile, Ahab and his chief minister Obadiah were scouring the land in search of food.

Obadiah was a God-fearing man and had secretly hidden and fed a hundred of the Lord's prophets when Jezebel ordered all prophets to be slain. And, while this brave man was searching for food, Elijah suddenly appeared before him and said, "Go and tell the king that you have found me."

Obadiah's reply was most significant. He said: "Wherein have I sinned, that thou wouldst deliver me into the hand of Ahab, to slay me?"

What did he mean? Read his own explanation. "It shall come to pass, as soon as I am gone from thee, the spirit of the Lord shall carry thee whither I know not; and so when I come and tell Ahab and he cannot find thee, he shall slay me."

Obadiah regarded the mysterious suddenness of Elijah's appearances and disappearances as due to the supernormal power of the spirit of Yahweh which transported him hither and thither.

Ezekiel assures us that he too was "lifted up and carried away by the spirit." And in the New Testament we read that "The spirit of the Lord caught away Philip."

Now, what possible meaning can such statements

have for those who know nothing of the findings of psychic science and are ignorant of the phenomenon of dematerialization?

These statements are natural enough to Spiritualists. They do not say that Elijah, Ezekiel, and Philip were transported by the spirit, that it must have been so because the Bible says so.

They merely say that, if these transportations occurred, they should cause no surprise because the same psychic laws are in operation to-day. Certain individuals to-day have known the experience of being dematerialized and transported many miles.

This fact inclines the Spiritualist to believe what is reported to have happened to "men of old time," and he has a *reason* for his belief. He has no belief in bibliolatry. But his knowledge of psychic science does make it possible for him to accept much more of the Bible than do the biblical scholars.

Elijah assured Obadiah that he would not vanish again until he had stood in the presence of King Ahab. With this assurance Obadiah went to the king and told him that he had found Elijah.

Who but a medium in close touch with the spirit world would have dared face a king who was hunting him to slay him?

The apostate monarch greeted Elijah with "So you are the man who has ruined Israel!"

Elijah boldly answered, "No, it is *you* who have ruined Israel, you and your family, by forsaking the commands of Yahweh and following other gods."

He then threw down the gauntlet and challenged Ahab to assemble the 450 priests of the god Melkart, and he would prove to them that Yahweh was all-powerful and that Melkart was powerless.

He suggested a trial by fire. Two altars should be built—one for Melkart, the other for Yahweh. A bullock should be laid upon each altar without kindling the fire beneath.

Each side (not very equal sides, one prophet of Yahweh against 450 priests of Melkart!) should then call upon its god to send fire from heaven, and whichever god sent the kindling would be the god worthy of worship.

From morn till midday, the 450 priests cried to Melkart to send fire, but all in vain. At midday Elijah taunted the priests with "Why don't you shout louder, your gods can't hear you, perhaps they are away on business, or asleep!" They shouted till evening, but no answer came; their gods were silent.

Elijah then dug a trench around the altar of Yahweh, arranged the wood, chopped up a bullock, and laid the pieces on the wood. He then saturated the altar, the pieces and the wood with water, and filled the trench with water. Such were his elaborate precautions against the suspicion of fraud.

He then prayed to Yahweh to send fire, "Let this people know that thou Yahweh art alone the Lord." And the "fire of the Lord" fell and consumed the pieces, the wood, the stones, the dust, and licked up the water that was in the trench.

The people were awe-stricken and fell on their faces crying, "Yahweh, he is God; Yahweh, he is God." They were convinced that fraud was out of the question.

A Bible-commentator remains unconvinced, and he actually suggests that Elijah only *pretended* to dowse the various parts with water. He believes that Elijah saturated everything with some inflammable liquid, probably naphtha!

We cannot but admire this commentator's honesty. He does not believe in miracle. He, like the Spiritualist, cannot believe in the arbitrary contravention of the laws of Nature. But he, *unlike* the Spiritualist, being ignorant of the laws of psychic science, of spiritual law in the natural world, tries ingeniously to explain away the supernormal element in the story of Elijah.

We wish all scholars were as honest as our commentator. For, how can it help anyone to believe that miracles were performed in Bible days but are never performed to-day?

The religion of the Bible is rooted in, and bound up with, the so-called miraculous; and, if to-day this miraculous element is absent, religion is moribund. Our commentator realizes this and is at pains to destroy belief in the miracles of the Bible in order to save our belief in religion.

What he does not realize is that all religion is rooted and grounded in the so-called miraculous, and that in explaining away the miracles of the Bible he is, unwittingly, explaining away the religion of the Bible.

The Spiritualist, on the other hand, is saving the Bible from destruction at the hands of the scholars, and is doing so by proving that the psychic laws which operated in Bible days are operative to-day.

Elijah's complete victory in the trial by fire led to the 450 priests of Melkart being slain. This enraged Jezebel, and once again Elijah had to flee from her vengeance into the wilderness. In utter prostration of body and spirit he threw himself down under a juniper tree and prayed that he might "die."

Yahweh's successful champion lost heart. He had reached the limit of human endurance. Yahweh had given him the courage to face Ahab and the 450 priests, but he had not prevented Jezebel from seeking to slay him. It was the last straw.

In agony of mind he fell into a deep sleep, and an angel touched him, saying, "Rise and eat." And there, beside him, was a cake and a jar of water. After eating and drinking he fell asleep again.

The angel came back and touched him saying: "You must take more nourishment, or the journey will be too much for you." So he arose and ate and drank, and in the strength of that food he went for forty days and forty nights to Horeb, where he took shelter in a cave.

While there he heard clairaudiently Yahweh saying to him, "What are you doing here, Elijah?"

He answered, "I am here because I have championed Thy name, for Israel has forsaken Thee and slain Thy prophets, and I, even I only am left; and they seek my life to take it away."

Yahweh then told him to go and stand upon Mount Horeb *before him*, to communicate with him. Elijah went, and suddenly Yahweh passed in front of him, but he could not hear what he said because a terrific storm drove him back into the cave.

When the storm had ceased, Elijah heard a still small voice, and came out of the cave. Yahweh then spoke to him, giving him a threefold commission: to anoint Hazael to be king of Syria, Jehu to be king of Israel, and Elisha to be his successor in the prophetic order.

And Yahweh encouraged his sad-hearted servant by assuring him that there were still 7,000 in Israel who were his supporters.

CHAPTER XXVIII

ELIJAH's sudden appearances and disappearances have baffled Bible-commentators. In our next psychic story we have another sudden appearance of this remarkably gifted medium.

Naboth had refused to sell his vineyard to King Ahab. So the King's wife, Jezebel, a veritable prototype of Catherine de Medici, bribed false witnesses to swear that Naboth had cursed God and the King and deserved to "die."

The lie worked. Naboth was stoned to "death" and the King took possession of the vineyard.

Elijah heard all about it clairaudiently from Yahweh, who commanded him to go at once to Ahab. What a command! Elijah was the King's enemy, and the Queen was seeking his life. But the man who has learnt to have a trustful fear of God fears no man.

Men of the world cannot understand the courage of those who are in close touch with the spirit world. They are staggered by the utter fearlessness of "men of God." The "man of God," Elijah, did not hesitate to "beard the lion in his den," but went post-haste to the King and pronounced Yahweh's terrible judgment upon him, "In the place where dogs have licked the blood of Naboth shall dogs lick thy blood."

And Ahab said, "So you have found me out, O my enemy."

Elijah answered, "Yes, I have indeed found you out. You have sold yourself in doing this evil. You shall be utterly swept away, and your Queen's body shall be eaten by dogs."

These predictions, although delayed on account of the repentance of Ahab, were fulfilled to the letter.

Now, what sense would there have been in Elijah predicting these judgments unless he had known, by psychic means—clairvoyantly or clairaudiently—that they would come to pass?

Another psychic story tells of Ahab's son, Ahaziah, who had fallen out of a window of his palace and been injured. He at once sent messengers, not to the prophet of Yahweh, but to the god of Ekron, to inquire whether he would recover or not.

Elijah suddenly appeared again, for a spirit-guide had told him of Ahaziah's fall and of the mission of the messengers, and had ordered him to go and meet them.

So Elijah intercepted them on their journey and said to them, "Is it because there is no God in Israel that you are going to consult the god of Ekron? Go tell the King that he will never again leave his bed, and will die."

The messengers reported this to the King, who naturally wanted to know what the man, whom they had met, was like. They described him, and the King said, "That is Elijah," and immediately sent a captain and fifty soldiers to seize him.

Elijah was sitting on the top of a hill, and the captain went up to him and said, "O man of God, the King orders you to come down."

Elijah answered, "If I am a 'man of God' let fire come down from heaven and destroy you and your fifty men."

And fire came down and destroyed them. The King then sent another captain and fifty men, but they too suffered the same fate.

A third captain and fifty men were sent, and this time

the captain fell on his knees before Elijah and said, "Pray spare my life and the lives of these fifty men your servants."

A spirit messenger told Elijah that he could trust this captain and was to go with him to see the King. And in the King's presence Elijah repeated word for word what he had said to the captains, and the King "died" as the spirit guide had predicted.

I am not concerned with the historicity of this narrative. I am only concerned to show that the narrative is rooted and grounded in psychic phenomena. This, and similar stories, are mere "fairy tales" unless the psychic interpretation be known and accepted.

To the narrators, Elijah's psychic powers were amazingly wonderful, and we are not surprised to learn that he knew on what day he would depart this life. Elisha also knew. And fifty members of the "guild of the prophets" knew it and told Elisha so.

By what means, other than psychic, could Elisha, the fifty prophets and Elijah know the day of his transition? They must surely have gained this knowledge clairvoyantly or clairaudiently.

Elijah evidently knew that he would not "die" in a natural way, so he sought solitude. But Elisha refused to leave him. So, accompanied by Elisha, Elijah paid farewell visits to the "guilds of the prophets," and then went to the banks of the Jordan.

Here Elijah rolled up his mantle, smote the water till it parted right and left, so that they could cross on dry ground. When they had crossed, Elijah said to Elisha, "Before I am taken from you, is there anything you would wish me to do for you?"

Elisha asked that a double portion of Elijah's spirit might rest upon him. But Elijah, not being quite sure of the extent to which Elisha was psychically gifted, answered, "If you see me *when I am being taken from you*, the blessing shall be yours, but if you fail to see me you cannot receive the blessing."

This probably meant that if Elisha could see clairvoyantly Elijah's etheric body building up while his physical body was dematerializing, it would prove that Elisha's psychic faculty was sufficiently developed to receive the blessing he craved.

Suddenly, as they walked and talked, a chariot of fire and horses of fire parted them, and Elijah went up by a whirlwind into heaven. Elisha saw it and cried, "My father, my father, the chariots of Israel and the horsemen thereof!"

The "*New Commentary*" frankly tells us that, "No explanation of the story is possible." Commentators maintain that it was either due to imagination or miracle, and they say that Elisha's exclamation meant, "My father, my father, you were a greater strength to Israel than all its chariots and horses."

But is that the real meaning?

Mrs. St. Clair Stobart has made a brilliant suggestion as to the psychic meaning of it all. It appears that elsewhere in the Bible "chariots and horsemen" are symbols of spirit messengers; the Bible makes that quite clear.

And "fire" may well be psychic light, e.g., the "pillar of fire" and "tongues of fire."

The writer of verse 4 of Psalm civ says, "He causes his messengers and servants to assume the form of wind and fire." And all psychic students know that the presence of spirit visitants is frequently heralded by a cold wind and psychic light or fire.

So this psychic story of the transition of Elijah, of

which "No (materialistic) explanation is possible," may yet be given a perfectly reasonable Spiritualistic explanation.

Elijah and Elisha were walking and talking when suddenly Yahweh's spirit messengers surrounded Elijah, who dematerialized in their midst. Elisha saw the psychic light which looked like fire, and felt the rush of wind which is described as a whirlwind, and caught a glimpse of Elijah as he was dematerializing, "being taken from him," and he exclaimed, "My father, my father, I *can* see you, and I can see the spirit messengers too."

It is interesting to notice that Elijah's mantle had fallen from him, which will at once suggest to psychic students that dematerialization had taken place.

The orthodox traditionalist may regard as fantastic this psychic explanation. But I submit that it does at least give a perfectly reasonable explanation, reasonable to all but those who have fettered their reason by unreasonably refusing to study the laws of psychic science.

In any case, the final word of the scholars that "No explanation of this story is possible" is not particularly enlightening, is it?

And when one remembers that Elisha was being put to the test, for Elijah had said, "Unless you see me when I am being taken from you, you cannot receive a double portion of my spirit," one naturally expects to read that Elisha *did* see him.

Elijah's translation took place in the very region where Moses was translated into the spirit world. And on the Mount of Transfiguration it was these two "deathless" mediums who were seen and heard by Jesus, and by those great mediums Peter, James and John.

I have come to the conclusion that the orthodox Churches do their people a great wrong in allowing these psychic stories of the Bible to be read in public without any explanation of them being given.

It is true that only a few listen to the reading of the Old Testament in church, on account of the length and "droning" of the Lesson. But what effect has the lesson on the few who make the heroic effort to listen? They are nonplussed.

The miraculous element in the stories simply dumbfounds them, and they feel, with the scholars, that "No explanation of these stories is possible." They therefore ask, "What is the use of our listening to all these miraculous stories when nothing like them is known to us to-day? It is sheer waste of time."

But what a difference it would make if Church people were told that the stories are not "miraculous," that there is no such thing as "miracle," that the stories are *psychic* stories to be psychically interpreted, and that what is reported to have happened super-normally in Bible days is happening to-day in London and throughout the world!

CHAPTER XXIX

ELIJAH's mantle and Elisha's bones possessed wonder-working powers—if we are to believe the Bible stories. But can we?

The Traditionalist says that we *can* believe them and *must* believe them, "because they are in the Bible." The Modernist says that we *cannot* and *must not* believe them, "because they are contrary to the laws of nature."

The Spiritualist says that we cannot and must not believe them with a blind and unintelligent faith merely "because they are in the Bible," neither ought we to disbelieve them merely because we are told "they are contrary to the laws of nature."

The Spiritualist knows that they are in no way contrary to the laws of nature, but only contrary to the laws of Modernists.

The fact is that material objects can and do become impregnated with spiritual forces, and it does not surprise the Spiritualists to learn that the mantle, which Elijah wore on his psychically, spiritually, magnetically, electrically—call it what you will—"charged" body, had itself become "charged" with supernormal powers; likewise the bones of Elisha.

"Good heavens," exclaims the critic, "these Spiritualists will swallow anything." Not so. Spiritualists feed on *facts*; they cannot therefore swallow the fictions of the critic.

When Elijah dematerialized, his mantle fell from him as did the winding sheet and napkin from Jesus when He dematerialized.

Elisha picked up the mantle and went to the bank of the Jordan. The guild of the prophets watched him, from the opposite bank, take the mantle and smite the water, and it parted so that he could cross.

They then bowed before him as the one on whom the spirit of Elijah rested.

Elisha thus became Israel's duly authorized prophet, the leader of the guilds of the prophets, who advised and warned its kings and made known God's will to the people.

On one occasion the Kings of Israel, Judah and Edom went to this medium and held a séance. The conditions were not very good at first, so Elisha sent for a minstrel ("for whenever a mistrel played, Elisha would fall into a trance").

His spirit guide "came through" and predicted that the three kings would defeat the Moabites. And it was so.

On another occasion, a poor widow who was unable to pay her "dead" husband's debts appealed to Elisha who, finding that she had nothing but a pot of oil, bade her borrow as many empty pots as she could.

She then began to fill them with the oil from her own pot, and found that it miraculously increased in the process. All the pots were thus filled. The oil was sold, the debts were paid, and the widow was able to maintain her family on the money that remained over.

We are also told of a man who brought Elisha a gift of some bread and vegetables. Elisha instructed his servant to feed a hundred men with the food.

"What!" said the servant. "Am I to set these few loaves and vegetables before a *hundred* men!"

Elisha answered, "Yes, for my guide tells me that all shall eat and be satisfied, and leave some over."

And "They ate and left some over."

Surely, if the "Feeding of the 5,000" is said to prove that Jesus was God, the "multiplication of the widow's store of oil" may be said to prove that Elisha was God.

For, though it might be argued that the feeding of a *hundred* men by Elisha was not so remarkable as the feeding of *five thousand* men by Jesus, the multiplication of the widow's store of oil was certainly as remarkable. I say this reverently and in order to stimulate serious thought.

Elisha made frequent journeys through Shunem, and a wealthy lady and her husband were kind enough to build a guest-chamber on the roof of their house for his use. In return for this kindness, Elisha promised that a son would be born to them the following year.

When the child grew up, he was seized by sunstroke and "died." Elisha restored him to life. Once again, we cannot help comparing the so-called miraculous powers of Elisha with those of Jesus. It clarifies thought to do so.

Through the psychic power of Elisha, the leper Naaman recovered from his leprosy.

A member of the guild of prophets lost the head of an axe, in a river. Elisha, by psychic means, restored the axe-head to the borrower.

The King of Syria warred against Israel and was astonished to find that his confidential plans were somehow or other made known to the enemy. He suspected treachery amongst his own officers. But one of the officers assured him that none of them was betraying him.

"It is Elisha, the prophet of Israel, who tells the King of Israel the very words you breathe in private," said the officer. Yes, it was the psychic power of Elisha that "saved the King of Israel not once, nor twice."

So the King of Syria saw clearly that his only hope was to get rid of Elisha, and he sent cavalry, chariots and a large force, by night, to surround the city of Dothan where Elisha was living. Early in the morning, Elisha's servant was terrified to find that his master was surrounded.

But Elisha was undisturbed, and bade his servant "Fear not, for they that are with us are more than they that be with them." Elisha then prayed that his servant might be given psychic vision. The prayer was answered and the servant saw that Elisha was surrounded by a vast host of spirit-helpers.

The Syrians descended upon the city, but Elisha prayed that they might be smitten with blindness, and in their blinded condition he led them into the heart of Samaria and presented them to the King of Israel.

Elisha then prayed that their sight might be restored, and they saw that they were captives. Now, who, with any intelligence, can believe such a story as this unless he be familiar with the supernormal phenomena associated with psychic science?

During a famine, which Elisha had predicted, the Syrians laid siege to Samaria. Things were so bad that the price of an ass's head rose to £10, and women ate their children. The king blamed Elisha for holding out delusive hopes of deliverance by Yahweh's might, and he sought to slay the prophet.

But Elisha's spirit-guide had already warned him of the king's intention. The king said to him, "Yahweh is the cause of all the trouble; what is the use of expecting him to help us?" Elisha answered, "Yahweh tells me that by this time to-morrow, in spite of the famine, food will be cheap in Samaria."

The king's adjutant ridiculed the idea, and Elisha assured him that, though he would see the food, he would not be permitted to eat any of it.

Yahweh now caused the Syrian army to be deceived by some mysterious sound which they took to be the noise of a mighty host marching to attack them, and they fled, leaving behind all their food.

The king gave permission to his starving people to plunder the Syrian camp, and, in the rush and crush, they trod upon the unbelieving adjutant, and he "died" in accordance with Elisha's prediction.

Now, who but a highly gifted medium could have foretold the famine, or known that the king sought to slay him, or that food would be cheap, or that the adjutant would be killed?

The next psychic story, of King Benhadad and his servant Hazael, reveals once again Elisha's psychic powers. The king was very ill.

Elisha was not far away. So Hazael, the king's servant, was sent with the urgent request that Elisha would "inquire of the Lord whether the king would recover."

Hazael took with him the medium's fee, which consisted of "specimens of all the rare wares of Damascus, as much as forty camels could carry."

But Elisha refused the fee. This munificent offer shows that Benhadad knew that Elisha could communicate with the Unseen and make known God's will.

When Hazael approached God's prophet, Elisha saw clairvoyantly, or heard clairaudiently, that the king would recover from his illness, but would be murdered by Hazael. This knowledge caused Elisha's face to become "rigid with horror," and he "burst into tears."

On being asked by Hazael to explain his emotion, Elisha disclosed his prevision of the atrocities which Hazael would perpetrate upon Israel. But Hazael showed no signs of shame at the idea of his own future depravity; indeed, it seemed too good to be true!

And he wanted to know how it was possible for him to achieve such greatness. So Elisha told him that "The Lord hath made it known to me that thou shalt be king over Syria."

Hazael returned to King Benhadad and told him that Elisha had predicted his recovery. But, the very next day, Hazael secretly murdered the monarch, and succeeded him as King of Syria as Elisha had foretold.

Is it possible for intelligent persons to believe that Elisha really did what he is reported to have done? It is possible on one condition only.

Intelligent persons must supplement their intelligence with a knowledge of what psychically gifted persons are doing in London and all over the world.

It is not a sign of intelligence to believe the "miracles" of the Bible while believing that no "miracles" have ever been performed since. It is merely a sign of abysmal ignorance.

CHAPTER XXX

ELISHA'S spirit-guide instructed him to dethrone Jehoram, the King of Israel, and anoint an army general king in his stead. Here is the story:

Elisha sent for a youthful member of the prophetic guild and told him to go to Ramoth-gilead, taking with him a flask of oil, and find General Jehu.

He was to ask for a private interview, pour the oil over the general's head, saying, "Yahweh hereby declares, I anoint thee King over Israel," and then run away as fast as possible to avoid being captured. The young prophet obeyed the instructions and found General Jehu, with the other generals, at a war-council.

"I have a message for thee, O General," he cried.

"For which of us?" said Jehu.

"For thee, O General," said the youth.

So Jehu rose and went indoors, and the prophet anointed him king, and the young man then fled for his life.

Jehu told his fellow generals what the young prophet

had done, and how he had said, "Yahweh hereby declares, I anoint thee King over Israel."

The generals at once acknowledged him as their king, and blew a trumpet blast proclaiming "Jehu is King."

Had the generals not known that the young prophet. the young medium, was a veritable mouthpiece of Yahweh, they would have ridiculed the whole idea. But in those days men knew that God made known His will through His own appointed channels, through the authorized mediums of the day.

Why was Jehu chosen to be king? Because he was the only man capable of destroying that abominable House of Ahab, and that incarnation of wickedness and idolatry—Queen Jezebel.

And he did destroy them, and thus fulfilled to the letter the predictions of the two authorized mediums, Elijah and Elisha.

And now we come to the last scene in the life of Elisha. He is passing into that spiritual world from whence he received all the help and guidance which he had given to God's people.

The King of Israel is at his bedside, shedding tears of genuine sorrow at the coming loss of the greatest patriot in the land, the saviour of the people.

It seems almost incredible to us to-day that a king should ever have visited a medium on his deathbed, and shed tears of genuine sorrow.

Kings and rulers no longer believe that God can speak through the lips of chosen servants. They ignore the channels of inspiration and guidance through which nations and empires could be saved.

Meanwhile the people perish for lack of vision. The rulers are blind. They grope their way, trusting to reason alone to guide them. But reason alone can give neither sight nor inspiration.

Yet, among their peoples are those who could, were their spiritual gifts recognized, give sight and guidance in the name of the Lord. They could become the mouthpieces of God to the nations, and save them from the clash of colour, creed and arms.

But neither statesmen nor State churches will recognize these would-be prophets of Church and State. They prefer to ignore or imprison them, unheedful of him who cried, "O Jerusalem, Jerusalem, which killeth the prophets, and stoneth them that are sent unto her!"

Prophets have not ceased to be sent, neither have stones ceased to be thrown at them.

A day will surely come when kings and rulers will shed tears of genuine sorrow at the deathbeds of God's chosen mediums. For, in those days men will know that the office of medium is the most sacred of all offices.

And there should be a public consecration of a nation's medium (prophet, seer) just as there is a public coronation of a nation's king. For the true prophet is of far greater value to the life of a nation than is a king. Yet we crown kings and imprison prophets!

The times are out of joint. Our sense of values is distorted. We hobble about on the crutches of creeds, customs and traditions, knowing nothing of the faith that could make us whole.

Notice now how even on his deathbed, that mighty medium, Elisha, made known God's will to the grief-stricken King of Israel. Remember that Israel's power had dwindled to insignificance through the folly and misdeeds of its prophet-forsaking kings.

Syria had reduced Israel's army to fifty horsemen and

ten chariots. And the King knew perfectly well that Elisha was Israel's only hope.

Little wonder that he wept and cried, "My father, my father, the chariots of Israel and the horsemen thereof!"

The dying prophet roused himself at this despairing cry of the King, and declared his undying faith in Yahweh's power to save the nation if only Israel would obey his commands. With his hands on the King's hands, Elisha bade him shoot an arrow towards Syria as a symbol of coming victory.

Who but a medium could have seen anything approaching a victory at such a time as this? How could an army of fifty horsemen and ten chariots defeat the mighty hosts of the Syrians?

But Elisha had seen clairvoyantly that the Syrians would first of all be defeated by another enemy, and thus give Israel time to regain its strength.

This symbolic act of shooting an arrow towards Syria gave hope and encouragement to the despairing King, for he knew that Elisha was in touch with the unseen powers and could make known God's will and purpose.

An uncrowned prophet of the Lord is of infinitely greater value to the life of a nation than a crowned king. Indeed, the value of any ruler may be accurately estimated by the measure of his obedience to the word of the prophet.

Kings were meant to be the appointed servants of the anointed prophets, and they will be so in the days to come.

Look once again at that psychic encyclopædia—the Bible.

When Hezekiah ascended the throne of Judah, he

found his people and country at the mercy of the King of Assyria, who had claimed suzerainty over the whole of Palestine.

The real reason for this was that the former kings of Judah had "done evil in the sight of the Lord" and had not consulted the Lord's anointed prophets.

Hezekiah, however, was determined to "trust in the Lord," so he at once asked the Lord's anointed prophet —Isaiah—to seek the Lord's help. Isaiah did so, with the result that "the angel of the Lord went forth and smote the Assyrians."

Later on, Hezekiah became ill and sent for Isaiah, who assured him that he would recover. But the King was so seriously ill that he doubted the prophet's word, and asked for some outward and visible sign that the Lord would heal him.

Isaiah said, "Let this be the sign unto thee from the Lord: I will cause the shadow on thy sundial to return backward ten steps." And Isaiah sought the aid of his spirit guide, who quickly enabled him to cause the shadow to return ten degrees.

"Utterly impossible," says the materialist.

"Not at all impossible," says the Spiritualist, who knows that equally amazing phenomena occur every day.

Sir William Crookes told me that, in his psychic laboratory, the pendulum of an unwound clock, which was hermetically sealed in a glass case, was made to swing not only from side to side, but backwards and forwards by purely psychic means.

He described to me how he had asked the medium if she thought it possible for her to make the pendulum swing (she was seated at the other end of the room).

She replied, "I will ask my guide," and, closing her eyes, she consulted him. In scriptural language, "She cried unto the Lord." She then opened her eyes and told Sir William that the thing could be done, and it was done.

Crookes's experience was by no means exceptional. All who have had the opportunity of thoroughly investigating the subject of mediumship have witnessed equally staggering phenomena.

I am well aware, of course, that the orthodox will regard as blasphemous my suggestion that to "cry unto the Lord" means to "consult one's guide."

But if I were to ask, as I have done scores of times, an orthodox priest of the Church what exactly is meant by "crying unto the Lord" he would say, "I think it means earnest entreaty in prayers."

Then, if I asked him to explain the words, "And the Lord said," he would say, "I think they mean the Voice of God in the heart."

But such interpretations render meaningless the Biblical narrative. And that is why so few Churchmen know anything about the Bible. It simply does not interest them, and they would deem it waste of time to study it.

On the other hand, students of psychic science delight in studying the Bible because it speaks a language they can understand, and corroborates for them their religious and psychic experiences.

CHAPTER XXXI

GREATER than the king and greater than the priest was the prophetess Huldah. She was little more than a girl. Her husband's grandfather was still alive.

Huldah was the "prophet of the Court," the acknowledged head of the nation, and her utterance of the divine will was accepted as authoritative.

It is true that Jeremiah was young, but he had been conscious of his vocation for at least five years. And there were other prophets who were exercising an authorized ministry.

Yet, at a most critical time in the history of Israel, when King Josiah wanted to know God's will, he consulted the greatest medium of them all—Huldah, the prophetess.

The most important event in the early history of Judaism took place in the year 621 B.C. Hilkiah, the priest, said that he had found, buried in the Temple wall, a book which was none other than the book of the Law of Moses.

He handed it to Shaphan, secretary of state, to read. When he had read it he took it to King Josiah and "read it before the King." The King was exceedingly alarmed for two reasons.

Firstly, because this book of the Law contained terrible denunciations of the neglect of Yahweh's Covenant.

Secondly, because the people were breaking the Covenant at almost every point.

So he at once sent his secretary, and the priest, to Huldah the prophetess to "inquire of the Lord"—which in modern language meant to "have a sitting" or "hold a séance."

At the sitting, Huldah's spirit guide told her that inevitable ruin would come upon Jerusalem for its sins, but that the disaster would be postponed until the King had passed away, for he had "humbled himself before the Lord."

This message they delivered to Josiah, who at once began to purge the city of its corruptions.

A king, a priest, and a secretary of state consulted the woman medium Huldah, the "prophet of the Court."

Why, then, did Paul forbid women to speak in church?

His rule has been quoted as if it were a precept for all time. But it was nothing of the kind. It was merely a temporary provision which had not applied in the past, and was certainly not intended to apply in the future.

How could it? Who would have the presumption to dictate to God and to say that He can only call and inspire *men* to become leaders of the Church's life?

Twice, when the nation's fate was in the balance, a woman, a "mother of Israel," had been called by God to do for the people what neither king nor priest could do. As compared with that golden age, the period in which Paul lived was one of miserable degradation for women.

When Jesus came, women had fallen lower than they had ever fallen before. The later Judaism had reduced women to a position equally unfavourable.

The Rabbis, even with the story of Huldah in hand, spoke of women as "a necessary evil." Jesus set out to rescue women from their hereditary disqualifications.

In Paul's day, no woman of virtue would ever make a public appearance, and the complete ignorance and want of education disqualified women from being leaders of the Church.

But the reasons which Paul gives for believing in the "subordination of women" are very amusing.

He says (I quote Moffatt's translation of 1 Tim. ii. 11): "A woman must listen quietly in church and be perfectly submissive; I allow no woman to teach or dictate to men, she must keep quiet."

That is humorous enough! But the reason he gives for his anti-feminist view is more humorous still. He says, "For Adam was created *first*, then Eve; and Adam was not deceived, it was Eve who was deceived, and who fell into sin."

But most humorous of all is what follows: "However women will get safely through childbirth if they continue faithful and loving and holy, as well as *unassuming*."

Paul had in mind the curse in Gen. iii. 16, "Unto the woman, God said, I will greatly multiply thy sorrow and thy conception . . . and thy husband shall rule over thee."

It was because of this curse that the Jews despised women, and the rabbis considered it a disgrace to be seen talking to them.

Why am I writing all this? Because it shows the origin of that insidious tradition, held by most of the orthodox Churches to-day, which causes them to reject the ministry of women. These Churches have consistently frustrated the spirit and intention of Jesus, and in so doing have reverted to the old Judaism.

I am now going to say something which I almost tremble to say. But it needs to be said. It is this.

The Bible rightly understood is the world's most precious treasure. The Bible wrongly understood is the most dangerous book in existence.

Who can estimate the damage that has already been done by the belief that every word in the Bible is the inspired word of God? That belief has drenched Europe in blood.

Who can compute the incalculable harm done by

1 Cor. xiv. 35 where Paul says, "It is shameful for a woman to speak in the church," and by Gen. iii. 16 and 1 Tim. ii., and by no end of other passages?

The superstition among us which leads Church and State to conspire together to imprison, repress, and ignore gifted mediums has its origin in an unintelligent Bible-worship. We are not only priest-ridden, we are Book-ridden.

And prophetesses raised up by God are cast down by the Church, and sent mute and unrecognized to the grave, because priests refuse to receive "the word of the Lord" through the mouth of a woman!

The irony and wickedness of the whole position is this: The Churches, claiming to be guided by God's spirit, have frustrated His spirit by laying down their own priestly rules and regulations for the guidance of the Spirit.

If the Spirit chooses to disobey the priestly rules by daring to speak to, or through a woman, the Church refuses to listen.

The Church has identified the work of the Spirit with holy orders and sacraments. And, according to this perverting superstition, a *man* is made a priest by laying on of hands, while no bishop would dare lay his hands for such a purpose on a woman.

The ordaining work of the Spirit of God is thus confined to *men* by *men*. And if the Spirit calls a woman to the prophetic office, she is told by the bishop that there is no such office—for women.

And this in spite of the revelation given through the prophet, "In the last days, saith the Lord, your sons *and your daughters* shall prophesy. I will pour out my Spirit upon all flesh, yea, on my servants *and on my handmaidens*."

The prophetess, Huldah, saved the life of her nation. She was inspired by God for that purpose. But the inveterate prejudice and ignorance of the Church of today would actually prevent God from saving the life of the nation if He chose to speak through the mouth of a woman.

In preventing women from discharging their prophetic office, the Church is committing a grave sin against the Spirit of God, a grave sin against the nation, and a grave sin against Mankind.

But apart altogether from the gravity of the Church's sin, the prophetic office is one for which Woman has exceptional qualifications by nature. Her mysterious intuitional powers, her sensitiveness, and her natural susceptibility to things spiritual fit her in an advantageous way for the office which the Church denies her.

Yet, while it is admitted everywhere that Woman is the more religious half of the human race, the so-called religious institutions have excluded her from communicating religious truth under the inspiration of the Spirit of God.

The Churches are attended principally by women.

How comes it then that this decay of the masculine element in religion is so marked? The answer is not far to seek. We may as well be frank about it.

From the cradle to the grave men are influenced far more by women than by one another.

And, as this is so, no mind can conceive the incalculable loss which the Church has inflicted upon men by refusing to acknowledge the ministry of women.

And when it comes to barring women from the prophetic office, and "quenching the Spirit" whenever a Voice from heaven speaks to her, or through her, no thought can measure the Church's sin.

God alone knows how much of the irreligion and unspirituality among men may be traced directly to the loss of the priestess and prophetess in the Church.

CHAPTER XXXII

THE BOOK OF JONAH is a psychic story, which tells how a selfish prophet disobeyed his spirit-guide, repented, obeyed and was taught a most salutary lesson.

No book in the Old Testament approaches nearer to the teaching of Jesus than does the Book of Jonah; that is why Jesus used the book. Every one should read it; it is a priceless treasure.

Unfortunately, all that the average person knows of it is that Jonah was swallowed by a whale, and that Christians are in duty bound to believe the story "because it is in the Bible."

Curiously enough, the whale-story is not in the Book. The story is of a "great fish" which swallowed a disobedient prophet, and the narrative is not quite so "fishy" as it sounds, for the sea does contain a fish, the cachalot, which could swallow a man, or even a small boat. And such a fact would give colour to the story.

But no fish is known that could provide a man with apartments sufficiently comfortable to enable him to produce the beautiful prayer which Jonah is said to have composed in his oily submarine. And surely no human stomach could stand the acrobatics of a fish!

Yet Pusey insists that all who deny the truth of the story are infidels. He informs us that Jonah was first thrown into the depths of the sea, where "weeds were wrapt about his head" (Chapter ii. 5) and that he was, as it were, rescued by the fish swallowing him.

But the author of the Book of Jonah was not dealing with historical material. His book is a midrash (an imaginative development of a thought or theme suggested by scripture) and belongs to the same class as Tobit and Daniel.

The book tells us that Jonah's spirit-guide had told him to go to Nineveh, the capital of Assyria, and warn the people that, unless they repented, their city would be destroyed.

The prophet Jonah lived about 750 B.C. Nineveh was destroyed in 606 B.C. The Book of Jonah was written about 325 B.C. So the book was written some *centuries* after the "death" of the prophet.

Well, the writer tells us that Jonah hated the Assyrians and loathed the thought of their being given even a chance to repent. He wanted to see them utterly destroyed.

So he deliberately refused to obey his guide, and thought he could escape from his presence by fleeing to Joppa. There he found a ship about to sail for Tarshish in Spain. Having paid his fare, he boarded it and went down below.

But his guide flung a furious wind upon the sea which so terrified the sailors that each began to pray to his own tutelary god to save them. Jonah was asleep in his bunk and the captain woke him and implored him to pray to his god, Yahweh, in the hope that He might save them.

Meanwhile, the thought had occurred to the superstitious sailors that someone, probably the passenger sleeping below, must be guilty and needed to be killed.

Curious idea! What would happen to a crew if every

storm they encountered demanded a victim from among themselves?

Anyway, they cast lots to discover who was the cause of the storm, and the lot fell on Jonah. So they asked him who he was, and he told them that he was a Hebrew who was fleeing from his spirit-guide, and from the God of heaven and earth and sea.

This magnificent designation of his God over-awed and somewhat scared the sailors, who were thinking, "How could this man have dared to disobey such a majestic Being?"

"What are we to do with you," they asked, "to make the sea calm?"

And Jonah, feeling very ashamed, said, "Throw me overboard."

But these pagan mariners had no wish to resort to so extreme a measure, for they admired Jonah's penitence and courage, and they rowed hard to get back to land. The storm, however, increased, and there was nothing for it but to pray to Jonah's God, begging Him not to punish them for casting His penitent servant into the sea, as they now felt bound to do.

Reluctantly they threw Jonah overboard, and the sea ceased from its fury. The sailors at once gave thanks and praise to Yahweh. Thus did Jonah's penitence and brave action have the effect of accomplishing a missionary end, though he himself was naturally unaware of it.

The key to the story is to be found in its moral—the impossibility of evading a spirit-guide and God's purpose; the universality of God's love and His desire to save all mankind, the selfishness and sinfulness of hating foreigners.

God had called the Hebrews to be His great missionary nation, but they had fled from this duty. So He had punished them by permitting Babylon to swallow them up in the Exile, though He released them later.

The "great fish" represents Babylon. Jonah represents the Hebrews, whom the "great fish" swallowed. Jeremiah employed the same figure, "Babylon hath swallowed us up like a monster; he hath cast us out."

But this allegory appears to have a double meaning. Mrs. St. Clair Stobart has pointed out that, just as a lion is the emblem of Great Britain, and a bear of Russia, so the emblem of Nineveh was "a fish and a house; four walls of a house, and a fish inside the house."

Thus, when Jonah entered Nineveh to preach, he was literally inside the "fish."

From within the "fish," and with hatred in his heart, Jonah warned the people by crying, "Forty days more and Nineveh falls!" He then went outside the city, made a hut for himself, and waited to see what would happen.

He hoped that the people would ignore his warning and afford him the exquisite pleasure of seeing them all destroyed. But the people repented and turned to Yahweh, and He forgave them and saved them and their city.

Now, if this be history, Jonah did what no other prophet, not even Jesus, ever did. For, in Nineveh, there were over a million people, who were converted by the prophet's ministry which occupied *one* day only!

But, as I have said, this is not history, it is allegory. It is the glorious announcement that God loves all men everywhere, and that when any man, anywhere, at any time repents, God freely forgives and reinstates him.

Jonah was enraged when he saw that Nineveh had

repented, and cried out to God, "I knew it, I knew it! That was why I disobeyed my guide and fled to the sea. I knew Thou wert a gracious and merciful God, slow to anger, rich in mercy, and ever ready to forgive."

Jonah hated the thought of bringing light to them that sit in darkness, and asked that he might "die" rather than live to see Nineveh saved.

The writer of the narrative was obviously an inspired man who, in later days, saw that his fellow-Jews were mercilessly embittered against their heathen neighbours. So he determined to proclaim, through the written word, his vision of the universal Fatherhood of God, His loving kindness and mercy, and thus imbue his fellows with kindlier thoughts towards their fellow-men.

He made the spirit-guide rebuke Jonah for the sinfulness of his rigid and exclusive nationalism, and ask him what right he had to feel as he did. His story then tells of the way in which the spirit-guide taught Jonah the lesson of his life.

The sun was beating down fiercely upon Jonah when the Lord caused a gourd, a shrub, to spring up and shade his head. Jonah was exceedingly thankful. But next morning, at dawn, his guide caused the gourd to wither away, and sent a sweltering east wind, and the sun beat on Jonah's head till he fainted and longed to "die."

The guide then came to him and said, "Have you a right to be angry over the loss of the gourd?"

"Yes," answered Jonah, "mortally angry"—by which he meant that he could see no righteous act in his guide permitting a useful and protecting plant suddenly to decay.

The guide replied, "Your judgment is right in the

matter of a mere plant. You are sorry about the gourd, though you spent no toil upon it, you never made it to grow.

"And am I not to be sorry for my children in Nineveh —not children called and chosen by Me to bring light to the Gentiles, but nevertheless my children whom I created and for whom I have toiled and whom I love."

We are left with the thought that God loves and cares for the vast populations of all the cities of the earth, that He is the Father of us all, that we are His sons and daughters, and are, therefore, brothers and sisters, and that it is our duty to bring light to them that sit in darkness.

CHAPTER XXXIII

The unknown author of the Book of Daniel was a Spiritualist. No one but a Spiritualist could have written such a book. It is a psychic story from beginning to end and shows how familiar the Jews must have been with psychic phenomena.

It was written about 165 B.C. under the pseudonym "Daniel" to encourage and inspire the Jews in their appalling tribulation under the Greek king—Antiochus Epiphanes—who had attacked Jerusalem, slain 40,000, and sent a similar number into slavery.

It is the latest book of the Old Testament, and was written some 300 years after Malachi.

The author was a brilliant visionary who saw that the hand of God had directed the whole course of Hebrew history.

Editorial Reviews of ***Psycho-Tropics***

"An engaging thriller with plenty of humor, good characterization, and a memorable villain ...." — *Kirkus Reviews*

"Marrying humor with suspense is not easy, but it comes across masterfully .... A truly enjoyable read." — *Judge, 23rd Annual Writer's Digest Self-Published Book Awards* (Award Winner in Genre Fiction)

"Clues are tossed out like bait, twisting and turning the storyline along .... The characters are brilliantly constructed .... The dark humor serves to lessen the tension in all the right ways before it heightens again .... Effortlessly captures the wonderful eccentricities of life in South Florida ...." — *IndieReader* (Official Seal of Approval)

"A genuinely creepy sadist is the high point of Box's dark thriller set in Florida in 1995." — *Publishers Weekly*

"*Psycho-Tropics* is like riding Pipeline with a hangover. It's jaw dropping, heart thumping and addictively exhilarating, but with a hint of disorientation, dizziness and an unsettled stomach. But by the end you'll be smiling ear to ear and bursting to tell your mates how good it was." — *Surfer Dad UK*

Order it on Amazon

Locations in *The Hiding Girl*

Memphis

ICONIC MEMPHIS is a bucket-list city to visit for too many reasons to list. The Bluff City regularly appears on lists of top worldwide travel destinations. But Memphis is also a city that struggles with high rates of poverty and crime that take a disproportionate toll on predominantly minority neighborhoods.

Much of the first half of the book takes place in the 38126 zip code known as South Memphis. Bordering downtown and the vibrant Beale Street entertainment district, South Memphis was ranked as the most dangerous neighborhood in the United States in one crime-data analysis. Below is one of the "death bear" memorials Emily asks Lucas about—teddy bear memorials where people were killed—this one at the corner of Vance Avenue and Orleans Street.

In order to convey his vision to his fellow countrymen, he transported himself, as it were, back to Nebuchadnezzar's reign in the sixth century B.C.; and, under the guise of "prediction," he expounded Jewish history as an unfoldment of the divine purpose.

Why did he withhold his name? Spiritualists will appreciate the reason.

The Law had become the absolute authority in Judaism. Revelation was closed and sealed. If a prophet received a message beyond or in conflict with the letter of the Law, he dared not deliver it, because the Law claimed to be all-sufficient for time and eternity.

Thus no room was left for new light and inspiration, or any fresh or further disclosures of God's will; in short, no room for the true prophet.

So, in order to circumvent the tyranny of the Law and the petrified orthodoxies of his time, this author was compelled to clothe his message in stories and symbols and to write under an assumed name.

To-day, we are still living under the tyranny of the Law and the petrified orthodoxies. Bishops, priests and Churches believe that revelation is closed and that no fresh or further light and inspiration can be received.

The Spirit that was to guide us into *all* truth has been confined within the narrow walls of orthodoxy. As it was, is now, but shall it ever be?

Now to the book. The author tells us that, when King Nebuchadnezzar had captured Jerusalem, he told his steward to introduce into his palace some of the best-looking and most intelligent of the young Israelites.

Among those chosen were Daniel and his three friends, Shadrach, Meshach and Abednego.

During Lent, there are thousands and thousands of

Prayer Book religionists who sing a hymn containing the words:

> "O Ananias, Azarias, and Misael
> Bless ye the Lord: praise him
> And magnify him for ever."

They delight in the tune, but not one in a thousand has the remotest idea who these persons were. Ask your Churchgoing friends and see how right I am.

The other day I asked the wife of a parson, and she told me that she had always imagined that they were archangels! And that is another of my many reasons for protesting against Prayer Book religion.

Its unintelligence is camouflaged by music and monotone. Words that are meaningless to the average worshipper are said and sung, and few ever realize how wicked it all is.

Shadrach, Meshach, and Abednego were names given by Nebuchadnezzar to Ananias, Azarias and Misael, and the hymn was sung by them when in the midst of the fiery furnace.

Well, the author tells us that Nebuchadnezzar had dreams which gave him sleepless nights, and that he summoned his court magicians to tell him what he had dreamed.

But they assured him that none but a god could tell a man what he had dreamed. "You must tell us what you have dreamed," they said, "and we shall then be able to tell you the meaning of it."

"No," said the King, "if you cannot tell me my dream you are in no way qualified to interpret it." And he ordered all his magicians to be "killed."

Daniel heard of this merciless order and asked his

spirit-guide to reveal to him the substance of the King's dream. And at night, in a vision, he saw the dream and was told the interpretation of it.

He then begged the chief executioner not to "kill" the unhappy magicians, but to take him in to the presence of the King, and all would be well.

Daniel assured the King that, while no magician could possibly tell him what he had dreamed, his own spirit-guide had revealed the dream to him. He then related it in detail and gave a full interpretation of it.

So awed and astonished was the King that he fell on his face before Daniel and acknowledged his god to be the God of Gods, and made Daniel prefect over all the sages and magicians.

Later, the King was foolish enough to set up a golden image and to command that all his people should worship the wretched thing under pain of being flung into a burning fiery furnace if they disobeyed.

The three Jewish youths—Shadrach, Meshach, and Abednego—refused to do so and were brought before the King, who tried to convince them that, unless they obeyed his command, no god could save them from being burned alive.

But with sublime courage the youths declared that, "There is a God able to save us, the God whom we serve, able to save us not only from the fiery furnace, but also from the King's power. But, even if He permits us to be burned, know this, O King, that we will never bow down before the Image which you have set up."

Nebuchadnezzar's face became distorted with rage and he ordered the furnace to be heated seven times as hot as usual. The youths were then bound and flung into the midst of the fire.

The King now became clairvoyant and he saw the

three young men quite free, walking in the midst of the fire, unscathed, and a fourth, who had the appearance of an angel, was with them.

He was more than alarmed and went at once to the door of the furnace, and cried out, "You servants of the Most High God, come forth from the fire."

And when they had done so the King exclaimed, "God has sent his angel to save his servants."

Now, none of this sort of thing could or would have been written had it not been taken for granted that the readers were perfectly familiar with psychic phenomena and mediumship.

The book now tells of Belshazzar, the next king, who gave a great banquet to a thousand of his lords.

At this feast Belshazzar drank too much wine, and, in a drunken frenzy, ordered his servants to fetch the gold and silver vessels of the Jewish temple (which his father had brought from Jerusalem) that he and his guests might drink out of them.

At that very hour the fingers of a man's hand appeared above the couch where the King was reclining, and wrote something on the wall.

It was a clear case of spirit writing, with which Spiritualists are quite familiar!

The King saw the writing. He also saw the materialized palm of the hand as it wrote. A clear case of partial materialization, with which Spiritualists are quite familiar!

The King's face paled and he trembled greatly while, in his terror, he cried aloud for his magicians to be brought in to read the writing and interpret it. But they could make nothing of it.

Daniel was then brought in, and the King offered him a purple robe, a golden chain, and the rank of "third within the realm" if he could read and interpret the writing.

Daniel objected to being bribed, and curtly told the King that he might keep his gifts, adding that he was able to read the writing and to tell the King the meaning of it.

Who but a great medium would have dared to tell the King the truth? But Daniel knew that he was fully protected by the spirit world.

So he told the King quite plainly that he had defied the God of heaven by recklessly bringing in the sacred vessels of His temple, and that God had caused the spirit hand to write "Mene, Mene, Tekel, Peres."

The meaning of this was: *Mene* (God has numbered the days of thy kingdom); *Tekel* (Thou art weighed and found wanting); *Peres* (Thy Kingdom will be divided up and assigned to the Medes and the Persians).

That very night Belshazzar was killed, and Darius the Mede received the kingdom and issued an edict forbidding the people to pray to any god except himself.

Daniel refused to obey the order and continued to pray to the God of heaven. He was arrested and flung into a den of lions, but "God sent his angel and shut the mouths of the lions."

And so it goes on. The book teems with psychic phenomena. And the readers were, of course, as steeped in the Spiritualism of their sacred book—the Old Testament—as, I trust, my own readers now are.

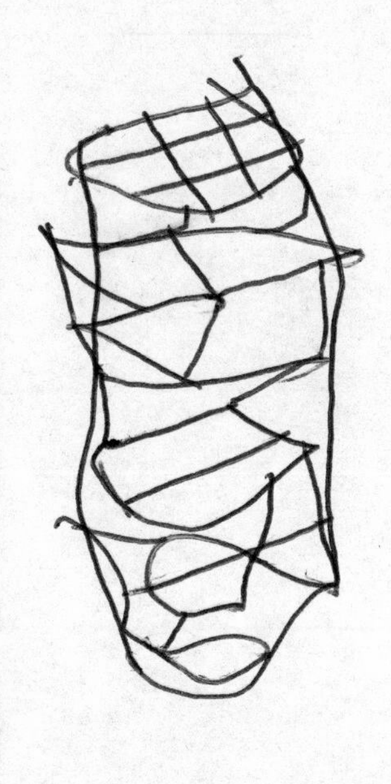